Whisky and Ice

Whisky and Ice

The Saga of Ben Kerr,
Canada's Most Daring Rumrunner

C.W. Hunt

Dundurn Press
Toronto • Oxford

Copyright © C.W. Hunt, 1995

Edited by Tom Kluger
Cover and design by Ron & Ron Design and Photography
Printed and bound in Canada by Webcom

The publisher wishes to acknowledge the generous assistance and ongoing support of the **Canada Council**, the **Book Publishing Industry Development Program** of the **Department of Canadian Heritage**, the **Ontario Arts Council**, the **Ontario Publishing Centre** of the **Ministry of Citizenship, Culture and Recreation**, and the **Ontario Heritage Foundation**.

Care has been taken to trace the ownership of copyright material used in the text (including the illustrations). The author and publisher welcome any information enabling them to rectify any reference or credit in subsequent editions.

J. Kirk Howard, Publisher

Canadian Cataloguing in Publication Data

Hunt, C.W. (Claude William), 1931–
          Whisky and ice : the saga of Ben Kerr, Canada's most daring rumrunner

Includes bibliographical references.
ISBN 1-55002-249-0

1. Kerr, Ben., d. 1929. 2. Smuggling – Ontario – History – 20th century. 3. Smugglers – Ontario – Biography. I. Title.

HV5091.C2H4 1995   364.1'33   C95-931839-9

Dundurn Press Limited
2181 Queen Street East
Suite 301
Toronto, Canada
M4E 1E5

Dundurn Distribution
73 Lime Walk
Headington, Oxford
England
OX3 7AD

Dundurn Press Limited
1823 Maryland Avenue
P.O. Box 1000
Niagara Falls, N.Y.
U.S.A. 14302-1000

For Jeffrey Webb Hunt

Contents

Acknowledgements

The idea for this book arose out of my research for an earlier book, *Booze, Boats, and Billions*. At that time there were no photographs or much information available on Ben Kerr, and I had to abandon the idea. Since then, George and Elizabeth Urban have come into possession of the Kerr family photographs and other sources have emerged concerning his death and career.

This book would not be possible without the cooperation and assistance of many people, and a few deserve special thanks, especially as some despite their advanced age were willing to grant me lengthy interviews.

In Hamilton, I am indebted to Kelly Thompson who managed the Pals hockey team until 1926. Also his wife, Lavina, who remembers the Kerr family when they were neighbours. The late Jack Morris Jr. who travelled the lake with Ben for almost three years was able to flesh out their life on the Lake. His daughter, Sandra Stokes, supplied the records of the Morris Boat Works. Paul Legall, crime reporter for the *Hamilton Spectator*, supplied some valuable leads. Ray Murphy, now in his tenth decade, provided a glimpse into how Kerr was perceived by his Hamilton neighbours. J. Ben Kerr had valuable recollections of his infamous uncle, and his son, Joel B. Kerr, provided legal searches of the various real estate owned by Kerr. Lynda Piper of Hamilton Municipal Cemeteries looked up information required to locate the descendants of those involved in the story, and Harry Cybulski provided me with information on the Plumbers and Steam Fitters Union, Local 67, of which Kerr was one of the earliest members. An unexpected source was the records provided by Ken Niepage, president of Adam Clark Company. It is rare to find a corporation which keeps records going back over ninety years, and they are to be complimented for doing so. The staff of the Special Collections Department of the Hamilton Public Library were very helpful, especially Brian Henley. The library is a treasure house of information on the Hamilton area.

The reference staff at Belleville Public Library were equally helpful in researching Kerr's activities in that area. Marie Wright, Elizabeth Mitchell, and Eleanor Jourard speeded up my research by their knowledgeable assistance.

Jack Choules at the Ontario Archives enabled me to gain access to the poison liquor files. Eugene Lang, a walking encyclopedia on music, helped me to reconstruct some of Ben Kerr's early career as a professional musician. He also shed light on the rules of polite soci-ety during the Edwardian age. Bob Button, who joined Corby's dis-tillery in 1924, provided a colourful glimpse into the way in which money collected from rumrunners was handled by the company. Purtell and Glen Quick of Brighton, supplied a sailor's view of Ben Kerr and his disappearance. Purtell's recollections of the man added another dimension to his character. The late Don Harrison of Trenton was a valuable source on Kerr's activities in Trenton, while the late Francis Welbanks, of Amherst Island, had stories about his more vio-lent nature. Aaron McGlennon happened to hear of my letter to the editor, concerning the finding of the bodies, and came forward to tell me his story. His daughter, Elizabeth Baker, made the contact and facilitated the interview. Ken Leavens, son of the barnstorming Walt Leavens, supplied valuable information and photographs relevant to the aircraft search for the missing men.

Finally, I must thank my niece, Ren Duinker, who assisted with the tedious research in newspapers and at Queen's University Library. Also, for her help in decoding the mysteries of the comput-er. Once again I am indebted to my wife, Mildred, for her patience, and for her evaluations of the prose.

Prologue

There are not many of them left. But the few old-timers who remember the days of Prohibition do so with a twinkle in their eyes, "Those were the days son, those were the days." For Canadians, Prohibition provided an opportunity to get rich by selling good Canadian whisky and beer to legally dry America at greatly inflated prices. Although the U.S.A. banned virtually all manufacture and traffic in alcoholic beverages after 16 January 1920, in reality the great republic was about as dry as the mud flats of the Mississippi at high tide.

American film and literature have popularized the colourful characters thrown up by Prohibition's "great experiment."

Canada's small population and the taboos of an uptight rural Protestantism prevented us from celebrating the equally colourful characters and events of our own past. This is finally changing. James Dubro and Robin Rowlands' excellent book on the crime czar Rocco Perri, who was the Canadian equivalent of Al Capone, reveals Perri to have been one of the most charismatic individuals in the annals of crime. Perri has the dubious distinction of making Hamilton – not Toronto – the head office for Ontario's mobs. Old established distilleries and breweries expanded frantically during these years to supply the huge American market. In the process, Canada became one of the world's leading producers of distilled spirits, known the world over for the quality of our rye whisky. Men like Rocco Perri and Ben Kerr were the point men who connected the titans of the distilling industry with the bootleggers to the south. Unlike Perri and most of these point men, Ben Kerr came from a solid middle-class family. Some branches of his family were more than just middle class. His brother, George, rose to the vice-presidency of Canadian Westinghouse. George's sons have been equally successful. James Kerr became president of Trans Canada Pipe Lines, and Robert Kerr was a prominent physician in Vancouver. One of Ben Kerr's great nephews is a practising lawyer in Hamilton, another is Bob Morrow, the long time mayor of that city.

How did a man with such impeccable family origins come to be the "King of the Smugglers"? Initially, Kerr was acting within Canadian law. As Harry Hatch, then-president of Hiram Walker-Gooderham and Worts, put it, "the Volstead Act does not prevent us from exporting at all. It prevents somebody over there [U.S.A.] from importing. There is a difference."

However, the legal distinction did not matter to the good burghers of Ontario. Prohibition was a moral issue. Once Kerr had taken the step of smuggling booze into the United States, it was an easy second step into violation of Canadian laws. For years, the career of Ben Kerr was kept under wraps by a newspaper sympathetic to the family. His mysterious and violent death on Lake Ontario has remained a subject of controversy. At various times, Kerr operated out of Belleville, Port Hope, Whitby, and Trenton. In each town you can find two or three different explanations as to what happened that dark night on the lake. But his direct descendants have all passed away, and photos and information, whose existence was not known, have now been made available. The strange story of this lone wolf of Canadian crime can now be told.

One

Double Death

"Behold. I show you a mystery."
1 Corinthians 15:20

The rectangular red-brick building with the steeply pitched green roof stands empty now. But in 1929, the CN train station in Brighton, Ontario, was an important centre of village activity. In the spring of that year, Len Wheat, a slight fair-haired youth of twenty years, and four bulky older men stood on the station platform on a blustery March morning. They were waiting for the train which would take them and the two wooden crates with human remains back to Hamilton. One of the crates contained just bones plus a hand with a barely discernible tattoo. The tattoo said simply, "Rose," but that was enough. Alf Wheat had had it tattooed on his hand in memory of his first wife. Len had been sent by the family to identify their father's remains. Three days later, the body of a second man had been found floating in the water nearby. Len Wheat had identified the body as that of Ben Kerr; the man the Americans called, "the King of the Smugglers."

Now the youth was taking both bodies back to their grieving widows. He did not mind the presence of the four policemen who had come down from Hamilton to investigate the two mysterious deaths. One officer had been a friend of his father and, like Len, the police suspected foul play. For the next sixty years, Len Wheat held the opinion that his father and Ben Kerr had been murdered on the lake by hijackers. Unknown to Len, the police suspected Rocco Perri, a headline-grabbing gang boss and Canada's first millionaire mobster.

The train with its macabre cargo arrived in Hamilton on Sunday morning, 31 March. The bodies were picked up by the Blatchford and Wray Funeral Parlour, who were to prepare them for the funeral services being held the next day. There was not much to prepare. The men had been missing in the lake for almost five weeks. In order to stop the growth of bacteria and absorb the odour, the mortician covered the bodies with topical powders containing dried formaldehyde and sawdust. He then placed each body, which were sealed in metal containers, inside the coffins.

The service for Alf Wheat was held from Blatchford and Wray's stately parlours on Main Street West in Hamilton. Louisa Wheat may have taken some comfort from the large turnout for her husband's funeral. Alf had been a popular man, a decorated war hero who remained active in the militia after the war. The service began at 2:30 in the afternoon. Two hours later the services began at the same parlour for Ben Kerr.

At the second service, the ordinary working men and women who carried the burden of poverty and grief on their slumping shoulders were replaced by men whose expansive girth and manner signified the satisfaction of success. The wives of these men had the upright carriage and confident smiles denoting respectable middle class.

However, on this day the smiles were muted, replaced by a disconcerting unease. The man they were burying was of their class but not of their kind. During his life, he had been a source of endless gossip and embarrassment. Now, in his manner of dying, he had added an element of mystery.

The service was conducted by the Rev. Doctor Samuel Russell who had married Ben and Louisa May sixteen years before. He had been retired for many years but had agreed to Louisa May's request in deference to her faithful attendance and support of the Anglican Church. Tall, grey-headed and stooped, the elderly cleric's presence commanded attention. He had been raised in the High Church, and wore the long, flowing gown and soutane particular to that branch of Anglicanism which aspired to Catholic symbolism. The Reverend Russell brought a dignity to the occasion, much desired by the widow Kerr and by the dead man's parents and brothers. After the service, the family accompanied the hearse to the Hamilton Cemetery for a burial ritual which, given the severity of the weather, would be mercifully brief.

The small knot of men and women standing near the hearse had to struggle to maintain the gravity of the event. Winds, gusting furiously, tore at their garments causing the women to clutch at their mandatory wide-brimmed black hats. The men tried to keep their fedoras on their heads with one hand while using the other to prevent their overcoats from blowing up under their elbows.

March had gone out like a lion. Hurricane force winds had torn off barn roofs, flooded rivers, and knocked down trees, causing hundreds of thousands of dollars in damage to southern Ontario. Of those present on that bitter, raw day, at least a few must have thought how appropriate it was. For almost all of his forty-five years, the man they were burying had led a tempestuous and stormy life. The Reverend Russell of Christ's Church Cathedral stepped a few feet in front of the rest while the pall bearers lined up to receive the casket from the hearse. George Halcrow, one of the six pall bearers, had been a popular public figure. He had distinguished himself as a Hamilton alderman and controller before moving on to a turbulent career in the provincial legislature as an MPP of the Independent Labour Party.

A stocky man, Halcrow grabbed the coffin rail firmly with one hand, holding his coat down with the other. This allowed the wind to tear off his fedora, sending it rolling down between the rows of headstones, where it played tag with the dead leaves from last autumn. Halcrow didn't give a damn about the hat or how he should be dressed. He was a working man, and had served many years as head of the plumbers' union. As an MLA representing Hamilton East for the Independent Labour Party, he had frequently battled the province's conservative establishment.

Halcrow and Kerr had been friends for over twenty years. They had first met as union activists at a time when unions were regarded by respectable middle-class folk as the enemy of democracy and the social order. Both had been rebels who had fought hard for the rights of the working man.

Of those present at the brief funeral, Jack Morris Jr. was probably the least surprised by Ben's violent death. The advent of American Prohibition had been a windfall, both for Canadian distilleries and for the rumrunners who delivered their product. For three years, winter and summer, young Morris had made big money, travelling Lake Ontario with Kerr and Alf Wheat. The younger Morris knew at first hand the risks involved in the trade, and was convinced the two men had been killed by becoming trapped in one of the fields of ice that often floated invisibly just below the surface of the lake. A few months earlier, Jack had given up the big money because he felt the risks had become too great. Consequently, he was still alive to talk about his adventures.

The most distinguished man at the funeral service was George Robert Kerr. Just two years older than Ben, the eldest brother had recently been promoted to vice-president of Canadian Westinghouse, one of the largest employers in the city of Hamilton. He and Ben had not been close for many years. George had worked his way up the corporate ladder. He belonged to the right clubs and fraternal organizations, was a member of the Dominion and Ontario Legislative Committees of the Canadian Manufacturers Association, was president of the Hamilton Chamber of Commerce, and had recently been included in the book *Prominent Men of Ontario*. Ben, on the other hand, had been a maverick and a law breaker. His headline making activities as a smuggler had been a major source of embarrassment, both to his wife and to his three brothers and their families.

It was Louisa May, Ben's widow, who had decided on the brief service. There had been no visitation, just a brief chapel service at the funeral home. The obvious presence of the Hamilton Police, both inside and outside the chapel, reminded the mourners that this was no ordinary death. Jack Morris suspected that the police were there because they had not ruled out the possibility that the two men had been murdered that dark night on Lake Ontario when they had gone missing. Although she seldom spoke of Ben afterwards, his widow maintained to the end that Ben had been murdered by his competitors.

She stood there now, serene and composed, her teenaged daughter standing self-consciously beside her. Both were dressed in mandatory black: long black gloves, black dresses modestly reaching to the ankles, and wide-brimmed black hats with veils completed the ritual attire. The black veil enhanced Louisa May's alabaster skin and large dark eyes. Not quite forty, she was easily the most attractive woman present.

With the pall bearers in position, Reverend Russell began moving forward in the direction of the open grave. The angry wind grabbed his words, hurling them into the void. But snatches of Psalm 90 drifted back – "Thou turnest man to destruction … thou hast set our misdeeds before thee: and our secret sins in the light of thy countenance."

The family would go to great lengths to keep the sins of Ben Kerr secret. Louisa May Kerr would, in the end, deny his very existence.

Two

The Strike and the Piano Player

John Benjamin Kerr was born in Hamilton on 29 February 1884. It was the apogee of the Victorian Age when family ancestry was as important to social position as wealth and power. The Kerrs were not wealthy, but they were certainly well bred. Ben's grandfather came to Canada from Northern Ireland and was the first fish and game inspector for the province of Ontario. He built an impressive home on the brow of Hamilton Mountain, and then constructed his own private road to gain access to the city. The house featured an elegantly curved hipped roof with irregularly placed dormier windows. The house would later become a designated historic building. Ben's paternal grandmother, a wealthy woman in her own right, was a member of the aristocratic Winslow family.

When Ben's grandfather died, the post of Fish and Game Inspector passed on to his uncle Fred, who held it until his death in 1898. During his early teenage years, Ben learned to hunt and shoot under the tutelage of his rugged uncle. These practical skills, while common among the rural population, were also popular with the solid middle class burghers and professional classes. Canada was then barely a generation removed from the pioneer stage.

When Uncle Fred died, the post passed on to Ben's father, Charles John Kerr. By this time the job had expanded to the point where additional men were needed. Eventually, Charles Kerr had five deputies helping him to supervise the counties of Wentworth, Halton, Lincoln, Brant, Peel, and Waterloo. The additional responsibilities meant a greater income and the family enjoyed a modest prosperity.

Like his brother Fred, Ben's father was an avid outdoorsman. These two men, who spent much of their lives in the woods and on the lakes of southern Ontario, passed on their knowledge of the weather and the outdoors to young Ben. At a time when accurate weather forecasts were not available to the public, Ben learned the skills involved in predicting storms, the onset of high- and low-pressure systems, and other weather phenomena so essential to the mariner and outdoorsman.

The outdoorsman was the aspect of Ben's personality with which most people were familiar. But in his early years, he was known for his talents as a pianist. He had probably studied the classics at the insistence of his mother, Helen, who came from a family which valued education. At the turn of the century only 6 percent of the population went beyond elementary school, but Helen's two brothers finished university and then went on to obtain their doctorates. His uncle, Benjamin Arthur Bensley, was a full professor of zoology at the University of Toronto and a director of the Royal Ontario Museum.

Ben was in the 94 percent that did not go beyond elementary school. A rebellious youth, he left school at the age of thirteen, spending the next two years in the highly regarded stonemason trade. Two years later, at the age of fifteen, he began his apprenticeship as a plumber with the Adam Clark Company which had offices, shops, and a retail outlet at 7 Main Street West in downtown Hamilton. Ben began his apprenticeship in 1899 and would remain with Adam Clark for a decade.

Repairing boilers, installing furnaces, welding pipes, all of this was hard work, but it was infinitely better than working as a factory hand or general labourer, most of whom were unorganized and earned about half the wages of a plumber or skilled tradesman. The average factory worker put in twelve hours a day, six days a week. As a skilled tradesman backed by a union, Ben worked a ten-hour day, five days a week, and "just" five hours on Saturday.

Local 67 of the Steam Fitters and Plumbers Union was organized in 1899. Ben was one of the earliest members. By 1909 he was the local's business agent, one of the more important and better paying jobs in the union. At about the same time, George Halcrow was working as a plumber with International Harvester and holding various positions in Local 67. In 1912 Halcrow was elected President of the local. The two men were nearly the same age, and both lived in Hamilton's north end, a largely working class area with a strong identity with the union movement. It was the age of the "robber barons," when workers were harshly exploited by owners and management. Government and police generally sided with the haves to put down the have-nots. Ontario had no minimum wages, no paid holidays, no unemployment insurance, and no right-to-strike laws. There was some government protection for women and children. They were not allowed to work more than sixty hours a week in factories, and the larger plants could not hire a boy under the age of twelve or a girl under the age of fourteen. Wholesale merchants and shopkeepers were less regulated, but were prohibited from working a boy under fourteen or a girl under sixteen more than twelve hours a day. The majority of the population was still largely rural, which was reflected in the provincial legislature. The farmers and the sons of farmers who sat in the legislature brought their farm work ethic with them, and had little sympathy for the idea of a minimum nine hour working day for grown men. There was some regulation of safety and sanitation conditions, but there was inadequate enforcement so that factory workers frequently toiled under conditions of poor lighting, unhealthy ventilation, and a general lack of safety precautions; industrial accidents were a regular occurrence. For the urban worker, life was a treadmill of grinding poverty, debilitating disease, and exhausting labour, broken only by the observance of the Sabbath – there were no paid annual holidays.

As a consequence of these conditions in the early years of the twentieth century, the industrial area of Hamilton (the north end) with its population of tradesmen, factory workers, seamstresses, and exploited immigrant labour, was a cauldron of frustration ready to boil over and scald its capitalist bosses.

Hamilton was an early centre of worker and union activity. The first working man elected to the House of Commons was an employee of Hamilton's Great Western Railway. Canada's first regional labour federation was organized at a convention held in Hamilton in 1872. It was organized by James Ryan, secretary of the Nine Hour League of Hamilton which championed the radical idea of a nine hour work-day. Daniel J. O'Donoghue, the first trade unionist elected to the Ontario Legislature, was a Hamilton printer.

In the early years of the century, Americans were investing more money in Hamilton than in any other Canadian city. Fuelled by cheap electricity and a plentiful supply of labour, heavy industry was flourishing. It was inevitable that the capitalists, believing in the doctrines of freedom of enterprise and the rights of property, would come into conflict with the emerging power of Hamilton's unions. One of the earliest and most violent confrontations took place between the Hamilton Street Railway Company and its workers.

In the larger cities, electric street railways, or radials, as streetcars were commonly called, carried more people to their destinations than any other form of transportation. Horse-drawn buggies were predominant in the villages and rural areas, and bicycles were at their peak of popularity in the cities and larger towns. Motor vehicles were still a novelty. The movement of large numbers of workers from home to factory or office could be done more cheaply and faster by streetcars than any other mode of transportation. A strike would be a considerable inconvenience to a great many of Hamilton's workers, both blue and white collar.

The union was demanding recognition, plus wage parity with their counterparts in Toronto who, at twenty-two cents an hour, were making four cents an hour more than Hamilton's tram operators. The company responded that, Toronto excepted, they were better paid than any other street railway workers. Despite several rounds of arbitration, the company refused to comply with the contract that had earlier been negotiated.

The Hamilton Street Railway Company had some of Ontario's most distinguished citizens on its board of directors. Their aim was to keep the railway running with outside workers and eliminate the union. They probably anticipated that an inconvenienced public would not support the strikers.

The strike began on 5 November 1906, and almost immediately became violent when C.L. Green, a company manager, stated to a reporter: "We are going to fight that union to a finish even if it takes two or twenty years. Our cars will be operated by non-union men and will never again be operated by these union men." The workers responded by stoning the railway cars as they attempted to move passengers through the city. The large glass windows made easy targets and many youngsters took up the sport. The company responded by installing wire netting over the glass, thereby protecting those passengers brave enough to continue traveling on the streetcars.

There were only about 180 strikers but they drew large public support, especially in the working class area of north Hamilton. "WE WALK" buttons began to appear on the lapels of Hamilton's citizens. In response, management hired about sixty Pinkerton police and strike breakers who were paid the then stupendous rate of $2.50 a day. They were quartered in the stone row housing across from the HSR depot on Hunter Street. Within hours of their arrival, the mob had stoned out every window in the place.

The violence escalated rapidly. It became a popular sport with the mob to plug the switches and one evening a mail car was derailed. A teenaged boy set fire to a blocked streetcar and was speedily tried and sentenced to six years in prison.

Premier Whitney was forced to act. He ordered the newly created Ontario Railway and Municipal Board to send its Tribunal members to the scene to intervene and bring about a settlement. They found their efforts hampered by a company determined to destroy the union at any cost, and a union which, though taking a beating, was thoroughly convinced it could win.

The situation deteriorated. Shots were exchanged between some special constables and strike sympathizers when a radial car derailed after striking an obstruction on Beach Road. When the police arrested stone throwers, they found their Black Maria surrounded by the mob and the prisoners freed. Tracks were dynamited on James Street North, and a hidden cache of dynamite was found. On 13 November, the press declared that it was no longer a matter between strikers and management but between order and anarchy.

The company badly needed the services of a public relations advisor. Whenever the public was thoroughly sickened by the strikers' violence, management would come out with a statement designed to further alienate the public. For example, on 21 November, a company official was quoted in the press to the effect that the company would decide who it would hire back, making it clear that the union leaders would be out of work.

Unable to control or restrain the violence, Mayor Biggar called on the government for troops to restore order. Soldiers and horses began arriving from Toronto on the evening of Wednesday, 21 November 1906. The next morning more troops arrived from the Wolsley Barracks in London, for a total of 177 soldiers. The officers were equipped with horses, swords, and .45-calibre revolvers. The men had long Lee-Enfield rifles mounted with bayonets. All the men from the Artillery and Dragoon regiments were equipped with horses.

The company asked Mayor Biggar to make the troops available to protect their streetcars, which continued to run despite an almost total lack of passengers. Fearing that such an action would further provoke the strikers and lead to even more violence, the mayor declined, instead he kept the soldiers confined to barracks. During the day, the north end of Hamilton was taking on a carnival atmosphere, with more and more people venturing downtown to view the excitement. But at night the crowds degenerated into acts of vandalism and violence. The flotsam and jetsam of society revelled in the deterioration of law and order, and the mob prevailed. Store windows were smashed and some looting occurred.

The strikers and the company continued to stare each other down. Emboldened by the presence of the military, the company announced that a new evening service for the streetcars would be inaugurated on Friday, 23 November. That evening each car attempting to run the gauntlet was met with a barrage of missiles from the thousands of men who had gathered downtown in support of the strikers, or as simply a break from a normally tedious and impoverished existence. The police lacked the numbers to deal with such a large and unruly crowd and inevitably the mob got out of control. Company offices at James and Gore Streets were stoned and all their windows smashed, store windows were broken, and the streetcar shed at Sanford Avenue was dynamited. When a policeman attempted to arrest a man for throwing a rock through a shop window, a crowd surrounded the officer and beat him to his knees. A fellow officer rushed to his fallen comrade's assistance and had to draw his revolver to hold off the attackers.

By 9 p.m., the company had withdrawn its cars from operation, but by then it was too late. The violence continued unabated. At 2 a.m., Mayor Biggar ordered the army to patrol the streets and gradually the presence of the armed and disciplined troops, combined with the physical and psychological exhaustion of the rioters, brought a temporary end to the violence.

After a riotous and drunken evening, thousands of workers were not expected to turn up for work. As a consequence, Saturday night promised to be even more violent than the previous night – already the worst in the history of the city.

The violence of the night before confirmed the Ontario Railway and Municipal Board Tribunal members in their belief that no negotiated solution was possible. On Saturday morning, two of them left the city, taking the train to Toronto to explain their action to a disappointed premier.

That Saturday morning, Mayor Biggar met with police Chief Smith who informed the meeting that his men could not maintain order and protect property without help from the military. Colonel Denison, the man in charge of the troops, had served with distinction in the Boer War (1899–1902) and was known for his flinty courage and flair for the dramatic. Facing the good burghers who ran the city, he coldly stated that he would need a magistrate at his elbow as it might be necessary to open fire on the crowd, and that a magistrate might be needed to testify to the legitimacy of the action. The prospect of the soldiers firing their rifles into a packed crowd of civilians put a chill on the meeting. Nevertheless, it was clear that keeping the troops in barracks was not effective and it was resolved to bring them out to protect the streetcars.

At 3 p.m. that Saturday, a cavalry patrol left the armoury and began walking its horses south on James Street. It was followed by others and, within an hour, all switches at the major intersections were under patrol. Some of the passers-by admired the smartly turned out soldiers, many jeered them, but the well trained and disciplined regulars simply ignored their civilian tormentors. In South Africa they had learned that the best tactic in dealing with a hostile civilian populace was to pretend indifference. But they were not indifferent, for they knew that in the evening they would be unleashed upon the mocking crowds. Psychologically, they were already preparing to deal with their tormentors in a fashion that would horrify many of the good burghers of Hamilton.

That same Saturday morning, Ben Kerr reported for work at the Adam Clark Company sometime before 7 a.m., spending most of his five hour shift welding and repairing a boiler. On his way home by bicycle, he noted the damage done along King Street and probably wondered if there would be many people present that night to hear him perform on the piano at John Seamenes' ice cream parlour. The taverns would likely be full, but would he draw a crowd from the respectable middle-class folk who patronized ice cream parlours? Perhaps the presence of the army would reassure them that the worst of the violence was over.

Kerr himself was not worried – perhaps he even looked forward to a confrontation. In the early 1900s, the police were generally regarded as the enemies of organized labour, and Ben was a seven-year member of Local 67 of the Plumbers and Pipefitters union.

Before leaving the family home on Mary Street for his gig at the ice cream parlour, Ben Kerr doffed his workman's cap and clothes and donned the three-piece suit of a gentleman entertainer. As a piano player, he changed not only his clothes but also his identity by assuming as his first name the maiden name of his mother. During the week he was Ben Kerr, plumber, but on weekends, he became "Bensley" Kerr, professional entertainer. The strong hands and long fingers of the plumber were also those of the professional pianist. It was a cold November night and Bensley Kerr completed the transformation by donning a stylish Don Carlos overcoat. Like all men's overcoats of the period it was black in colour. Its narrow lines emphasized Bensley Kerr's considerable height. Looking elegant and distinguished, Kerr walked down the street, little knowing that he was on his way to becoming a local folk hero among Hamilton's working classes.

Three

The Riot Act

By Saturday afternoon the rumour mills of Hamilton throbbed with the news that the Sheriff was going to read the Riot Act (an order of the mob to disperse) from the steps of City Hall. Far from dispersing, thousands of the curious showed up downtown. Clearly, very few of the citizenry had any idea what to expect once the act had been proclaimed.

At precisely 7:15 p.m., a small knot of men left City Hall (then near Eaton's) and walked out to the steps overlooking James Street. They were greeted with a thunderous roar of a crowd of three thousand, which surged toward the steps. A thin line of police, backed by soldiers held them in check. The greying bearded figure of Sheriff Middleton, dressed in formal black and carrying a cane, stepped forward; he was holding a copy of the criminal code. To his left stood the portly Mayor Biggar. To his right, police Chief Smith stood ramrod straight, staring down at the crowd with the eyes of a basilisk. For three endless weeks, his force had been subjected to insult, humiliation, and even physical abuse. Retribution was at hand.

Slightly forward of these three men, sitting easily on a prancing bay stallion, Colonel Septimus Julius Augustus Denison waited to give the signal to his troops. Mayor Biggar raised his hand in a futile attempt to quiet the crowd, then nodded to Sheriff Middleton who proceeded to read the Riot Act. The message was brief and ominous:

> His Majesty the King charges and commands all persons being assembled immediately to disperse and peaceably to depart to their habitations or to their lawful business upon the pain of being guilty of an offence for which upon the conviction, they may be sentenced to imprisonment for life. God Save the King.

The unruly crowd drowned out the words, but the letter of the law had been observed. Chief Smith signalled his men who immediately moved forward into the crowd, nightsticks thudding on shoulders, arms, and heads. The dragoons followed, the mounted soldiers beat-

ing everyone in their path with the broad side of their swords, their
horses swinging left and right, knocking into the dirt those unable to
get clear. Behind them came the foot soldiers. Their long rifles with
their menacing ten-inch bayonets were held in front and pointed forward. They used the butts of their rifles on any stragglers missed by
the police and dragoons. The crowd dissolved as people tried desperately to escape from the clubs and rifle butts.

Within a minute a hundred people of both sexes lay bleeding on the
ground. One alderman, watching the proceedings from the safety of an
office overlooking James Street, was aghast at what he saw. He declared
that the police charged the crowd, "like a lot of Russian soldiers."[1]

Colonel Denison was in his element, prancing among the soldiers, shouting "give it to them men, give it to them."[2] He later complained that his soldiers had held back and only did their job after the
crowd had stoned the dragoons' horses.

With the City Hall crowd dispersed, the police and military proceeded to methodically clear the downtown area, interpreting the
Riot Act literally; you had to be in your home or at work otherwise
you were breaking the law. Jones Lewis was on his way to work at the
Hamilton *Herald* when he was pursued by the military right into the
newspaper's editorial offices. A choir practice at Knox Church was
broken up as it was an illegal assembly while the act was in effect. The
innocent choristers left in confusion and disarray.

Despite these actions, the mob threatened once again to take control. Policemen, soldiers, their horses, and trolley cars continued to be
stoned. Two hours after the reading of the act, a mob had stopped a
trolley car at King and Walnut streets, and was threatening the lives
of the car's seven occupants. They were saved by the timely arrival
of police and soldiers.

At about the time this action was taking place, Ben Kerr was
walking the few blocks from his home on Mary Street to 123 King
Street West, where the proprietor, John Seamenes, and a surprisingly large group of patrons were awaiting the evening's entertainment. They may have thought that, within the confines of a private business, they were safe from the police, soldiers, and the ruf-
fians who crowded the streets. Many young matrons were there
with their husbands. No doubt, there were some unattached young
women present. They would be suitably under escort by a brother,
parent, or other family member who could qualify as a chaperon
and preserve their reputation. Victorian morality was just beginning to loosen its grasp on the behaviour of middle-class women.

Kerr arrived, elegantly dressed in a three-piece suit, gold watch chain across his slim waist, and a fashionable cravat knotted under a wing collar. Over this he wore a Don Carlos overcoat which was a double-breasted, waisted coat, deeply pleated in the back. The whole effect dramatically set off by a wide-brimmed, black felt hat, a type usually worn by intellectuals and musicians. Once inside John Seamenes' ice cream parlour, Kerr paused before removing his overcoat. He wanted the patrons to see that he had walked there with a "We Walk" button blatantly pinned to his outer garment.

A murmur of approval ran through the crowd, and a few hands clapped enthusiastically. More than a few of the young women present felt a flutter of heart and breath, for Bensley Kerr cut a dashing figure. He was tall – over six feet – blue eyes, a fine roman nose, and a full, rather sensuous mouth. The patrons had come to hear him play the romantic salon music so popular with the masses at that time. Mellow, saccharine sweet pieces such as "Mother's Wish," "Dying Poet," and Claude Debussy's "Claire de Lune." Bensley Kerr, aspiring musician, played them all. But occasionally his rebellious nature broke through and he startled his audience by playing a bit of ragtime, a disturbing new music beginning to percolate up from New Orleans. This did not always endear him to his employers, but Kerr was a hard man to constrain. He was not one to take orders from others.

He was in the middle of a ragtime piece, "doing tricks" the press called it, when three soldiers appeared in the doorway. Sergeant Youngman and two troopers were there to clear the doorway of the crowded restaurant but they met unexpected resistance. They had succeeded in driving their resistors into the restaurant when the proprietor rushed out from behind his counter shouting that "he was a Greek and no Canadian soldier could invade the sanctitude of his premises."[3] Seamenes, his hair bristling, struck at Youngman with a club. Kerr had come out from the back room where he had been performing and proceeded to wrestle the rifle out of Youngman's hands, passing it over his shoulder to the crowd behind him where it disappeared. Youngman and the troopers hastily retired from the fray to get reinforcements.

A short time later, a Corporal Raymond entered the restaurant with two other soldiers to arrest Bensley Kerr. When they confronted him in the back of the store, Kerr picked up his piano stool, felled two of his would-be arresters, and dashed out the door. A company of soldiers was waiting for him around the corner. Kerr was wearing patent leather shoes and when he tried to reverse direction he fell right into the arms of the soldiers. Along with thirty-two other "rioters," Kerr was lodged in jail without bail. Of the thirty-two arrested, most were charged with throwing stones or other minor crimes, only Kerr and one other were charged with assaulting a soldier or policeman.

The next day dawned peacefully on the battered city. The street-cars ran sedately. Store owners swept up glass or went to church. The soldiers paraded for divine service at the Armories. The strikers attended two church services, in the morning at St. George's, and in the evening at James Street Baptist.

Reporters found Colonel Denison lounging in the Officers' Mess of the Thirteenth Regiment. The Colonel recounted how he had the plea-sure of a little action himself when, just before the Riot Act was read, a buggy had been driven furiously by him, forcing his horse to give ground. Not one to take such slights lightly, he took after the buggy himself. When the driver cut at him with his whip, Denison chuckled that he, "wrenched the whip from his hand, and I need hardly say that for the next hundred yards, that whip swung around the heads of those two men with all the force I could put into it. It was accompanied by the most pitiful shrieks it has ever been my pleasure to hear."[4]

The Colonel commended the police but criticized the soldiers for holding back. He stated that if they had to be called out again he could assure the reporters that they would not act with such forbearance. He went on to say: "I assume the position that after the Riot Act is read, no respectable, law abiding person will be found on the streets. If we are called out tomorrow, we will clear the streets at any cost, and people, for their own safety, had better be in their own homes."[5]

Fortunately, Denison did not get the opportunity. Hamiltonians had been shocked by the violence. Also, it was clear to the underclass responsible for much of the riotous activity that any repeat of their actions would be met with the harshest of force. Strikers and man-agement agreed to abide by the decision of the Ontario government's tribunal. The strike ended on 29 November and streetcar service resumed. Both sides could claim a measure of victory. The company was forced to recognize the union, but wages and working conditions were to remain the same.

But the company's earlier intransigence, and the severity of the police attacks – some of them on innocent citizens going about their business – turned public opinion in favour of the strikers. Those in jail awaiting trial hoped that this sympathy would translate into lenient sentences.

With the issue of the strike settled, there was much popular interest in the trials of the rioters, especially that of John Benjamin Bensley Kerr whose family was well known and respected.

On 12 December, the Grand Jury proceeded to try all but one of the defendants. Two charges were laid against Ben Kerr; one of assaulting a peace officer, and the other of escaping from custody. Seamenes was charged with assaulting a police officer.

Their trial began on 14 December 1906, with both men pleading not guilty. The Crown called several witnesses. Sergeant Youngman testified that he had arrived at the restaurant at about ten in the evening, and that Kerr had told Seamenes, "to hit him [the soldier] with a club," and that Seamenes and Kerr had struck him on the arm. Kerr, he stated, had grabbed the gun and passed it back into the crowd where it disappeared.

Seamenes defense was that he was protecting his customers from the bayonet that Youngman was pointing in a threatening manner. Youngman denied this in his testimony but another soldier, a Private Smith, confirmed the testimony of Seamenes. Several of the patrons present that night testified they had reason to fear a bayonet charge.

The next day a number of young women came forward to testify on behalf of Kerr. One, a Mrs. McLean, stated that she had been in the store both times when the soldiers had entered and that Mr. Kerr had not struck any soldier. She had seen him pick up the piano stool but he had merely placed it on the counter. The testimony of the soldiers was obviously in direct conflict with that of the ladies and with the other witnesses in the store. As often happens in such confrontations, truth was sacrificed to partisanship. According to family legend, Kerr did knock down two soldiers with his piano stool.

Kerr testified in his own defense showing the judge his coat with bayonet cuts in it. He directly refuted the testimony of the soldiers. When Judge Snider pointed out the contradictions between the defendant's statements and that of the soldiers, Kerr suggested that the soldiers' testimony, "was all a dream."[6] Although lacking in formal education, John Benjamin Kerr was not intimidated by the courts or by officialdom in general.

The jury took about twenty minutes before dismissing the charges against Kerr. Hamilton at that time was about 95 percent Anglo-Saxon, which may explain why that same jury found Seamenes guilty of assaulting a peace officer.

The next day, the *Hamilton Herald* in an unprecedented action commented on the guilt and sentencing of John Seamenes. The paper had been more sympathetic to the strikers than its rival, the *Spectator*, but by editorializing on the upcoming sentence of Seamenes, the *Herald* was clearly in contempt of court. The editorial read in part, "that storekeeper who struck a soldier on the arm to save one of his employees from being stabbed by the soldier's bayonet, may be technically guilty of a serious offence but he is no criminal and the *Herald*, for one, thinks he is worthy of admiration rather than punishment."[7] The *Herald* was aware that Seamenes could receive as much as two years in prison.

Judge Snider castigated the newspaper and its editors for this breach of the law, but took no further action against the *Herald*. The atmosphere in the city was tense and the strike not fully settled. No doubt the judge did not wish to further aggravate relations between the authorities and the community at large.

Sentencing took place on 20 December 1906, just four days after the grand jury had brought in "true bills"* against the defendants. But the grand jury also recommended that the judge deal leniently with those found guilty. This recommendation was generally ignored. The man accused of brandishing his buggy whip at Colonel Denison and striking Major Dore with it, received eighteen months in Central Prison. Two others found guilty of being in unlawful assembly were each sentenced to one year in Central Prison. Several witnesses testified to the sterling character of John Seamenes and to his contribution to the community as a hard working business man. He received two months less the two weeks he had already spent in jail.

Ben Kerr was only twenty-two years of age at the time of the Street Railway Strike, but his actions against the militia men and his subsequent trial made him a popular figure in certain working-class circles in the north end of Hamilton. The police and the courts were viewed by organized labour as the allies of capital and the enemies of labour. The young plumber's defiance of the authorities and his conduct in court marked him for promotion within the ranks of organized labour. Three years later, Ben Kerr had advanced to the rank of business manager in Local 67 of the Plumbers and Steamfitters' union. But his brush with the courts confirmed Kerr in his opinion that he could successfully defy the law and the authorities enforcing it.

---

*True bills are brought in when the grand jury finds there is sufficent evidence to support a bill of indictment, thereby clearing the way to try the defendant.

Four

Power Boats and Politics

The first decade of the twentieth century was a period of enormous growth for Canada, especially for Hamilton. The population of the city doubled, and its harbour became the second busiest in Canada, surpassed only by Montreal.

Hard working and thrifty, Ben Kerr watched these developments and made preparations to take advantage of the growing need for boat houses in Hamilton harbour. As a teenager, the young Kerr had frequently accompanied his father when the latter had used motor-boats to check on illegal fishing. Perhaps it was the excitement of these trips which led to Ben's interest in the sport of power boating.

In the spring of 1905, an article in the now-defunct Hamilton *Times* noted that power boat racing was surpassing skiff (sail boat) racing in popularity, and that Hamilton boat builders were receiving many more orders for powerboats than for sailboats.[1] The gasoline engine was about to transform transportation on land and water. Kerr was fascinated with the new technology and would become an expert on marine engines.

The largest boat builder in Hamilton was Henry Bastien who employed twenty full-time workers, and had an invested capital of $25,000. In the early 1900s, he could build a customer a thirty-three foot gasoline launch for $310 (motor extra), or a twenty-eight foot cabin cruiser with Sterling engine for about $3,000.[2]

In addition to Bastien, there were six other boat building concerns, including John Morris, James Massie, the Robertson Brothers, the Weir Brothers, William Johnson, and T.W. Jutten. In the spring of 1905, they were so busy that several stated they could not keep up with their orders. The increasing popularity of gasoline-powered pleasure boats created a need for more boat houses, but only a few of the builders responded to this demand. H.L. Bastien had the most complete facility which included a two-storey building for boat repair, a two-storey boat works for the building of new boats, and units for the storage of forty pleasure craft.[3]

Ben Kerr was earning about a thousand dollars a year as a plumber. This income was supplemented by another $125 from his position as business agent for the union. He earned additional income from piano playing. Unlike his older brother who had married in 1906, Ben had remained a bachelor and saved money by boarding at his parents' home. In June of 1910, he had saved enough to purchase a waterfront lot on Bay Street North for $350. The following year, he purchased the adjoining lot and, in June, began construction of a dock and fifty boat lockers, making him the largest renter of boat storage lockers in the city. To raise the money to pay for their construction, he placed a mortgage on his properties for two thousand dollars.[4] Unfortunately for Kerr, Bastien and others soon increased the number of their boat storage units. This drove down the rents that could be charged and Kerr discovered that his rentals barely covered his mortgage payment. Nevertheless, the boat houses were to prove a shrewd long-term investment.

A fiercely ambitious man, Ben Kerr had little time for romance. Working fifty-five hours a week at plumbing, taking care of Local 67's business in his off hours, and playing the piano on Saturday nights, did not leave much time for matters of the heart. Nevertheless, sometime in 1910 or 1911, he met Louisa May Byrens and fell in love.

They probably met at one of the better hotels when Ben was performing. Louisa May was a music lover, and taught piano out of her parents' home at 58 Magill Street. Edwardian morality required that a respectable middle-class woman must have a chaperone to go out in the evening. One of her older brothers would have been enlisted to fill that requirement for her. Once engaged Louisa and Ben could be seen together without a chaperone, but it was not considered appropriate for her to continue working. After 1910, she no longer advertised herself as a piano teacher.

They made a handsome couple. A stylish dresser, Ben was tall, slim, and broad shouldered, with sandy-brown hair and piercing blue eyes. Five years younger than Ben, Louisa May's most prominent features were her soft brown eyes, mother of pearl complexion, and voluptuous mouth. Her gentle femininity complemented Ben's aggressive charm.

They were to be married at the bride's home on 28 August 1912. However, business success and the prospect of marriage had not tamed Ben's fiery nature nor his resentment of authority. In March 1912, just a few months before he was to be married, Ben Kerr got into an argument with a patrolman outside his parents' home and was charged with disorderly conduct. The trial was held on 1 April, with

Magistrate Jeffs presiding. The Hamilton *Daily Times* reported on Kerr's conduct of his own defence, noting, "the systematic way in which Kerr took up his stand where the Crown Attorney usually holds forth and fired questions at the witnesses and tried to tangle them up in their evidence, amused the lawyers and court officials." Magistrate Jeffs failed to see the humour in the young man's defiance of court protocol, and when Kerr declared that the constables should be charged with perjury, he replied, "that shows your antagonistic character and manner ... You're fined two dollars." Ben responded by appealing the decision.[5]

The court case was a minor blemish on a steadily improving success story. His boat houses were fully rented, plumbers' wages were rising, and his brother, George Kerr, had been promoted to treasurer of Canadian Westinghouse. Before the wedding, Ben bought his bride-to-be a beautiful and expensive pearl pendant.

At the wedding, Louisa May was lovely in a dress of ivory duchess satin with rose-point lace and pearl trimming. Guests arrived from Toronto, Montreal, Stratford, Elmira, and other centres. After the wedding dinner, the couple departed by train on a leisurely trip to Penetang, Madawaska, and other points in the north country. They would be "at home" to their friends after 1 October. Following the rules of polite society, the new Mrs. Kerr had calling cards printed up for distribution to those friends whom she and her husband would welcome to their home. The manners and rules of society were quite clear. If you did not receive a card you did not call nor expect that you would be called. Manners also required that the lady not print her name but her husband's Christian name on the card.[6] Louisa May had her card printed as Mrs. Bensley Kerr. She clearly preferred to regard her husband as Bensley Kerr, pianist, rather than as Ben Kerr, plumber.

Their honeymoon trip to Ontario's northern wilderness was no doubt planned by Ben who had an abiding love of the outdoors. Louisa May would have preferred the agenda followed by Ben's brother, George, who took his bride to New York City on their honeymoon.[7] But Ben was a dominant and forceful personality and, as befitted a woman's place in her age, Louisa May deferred to her husband's wishes. This early disagreement was a portent of future conflict in the marriage.

On their return, the couple took up residence at her parents' two-storey home at 58 Magill Street. They would remain there for a year until the summer of 1913 when their daughter, Helen, was born. She was named after Ben's mother, a tiny dynamo from whom Ben had inherited his love of music.

The birth of their daughter crowded the house at Magill Street. Most skilled tradesmen could afford their own home, but Ben's financial resources were stretched to their limit by the building of the boat houses. He found a house for rent near them. It was a large three-storey home at 429 Bay Street North, just a few minutes walk from his business and from his old plumbing buddy and union friend, George Halcrow.

Halcrow had married Georgina Renton in 1904 and shortly after moved into a modest house at 379 Bay Street North. The two men had been on the picket lines together during the plumbers' strike in 1907, and had held various positions in the union.[8] Their paths diverged after 1912 when Kerr gave up his position as business agent in order to devote more time to his marine garage and boat storage business, while Halcrow took on the duties of union president, a post he would hold for three years.

Considering their lack of formal education, both men were well spoken, but where Kerr was fiery and explosive, Halcrow was genial and persuasive. Given his talents, it is not surprising that Halcrow moved into politics. In the summer of 1915, an alderman resigned from Hamilton City Council. The city had a strong labour contingent and they were successful in getting George Halcrow appointed to fill the vacant seat. The position was unpaid but Halcrow's ambition was not monetary. Moreover, public life gave him a better platform from which to argue the interests of the working man. In December of 1916, he stood for election as one of two alderman who would represent Ward Five. There were several candidates for the two posts. A local merchant led the polls, but Halcrow managed a close victory over the other two candidates. He was now in a position to push labours' point of view concerning the Great War and the problems it was causing the working man.

The First World War was raging over Europe, and Canada, as a leading member of the British Empire, was deeply involved. All across English-speaking Canada, young men had flocked to join the army and serve for "King and Country." Quebec's leaders had regarded the conflict as a struggle for European hegemony, a war between the British and German empires (a view now generally accepted by historians). This refusal by Quebecers to respond to the demands of British patriotism created much anger in the rest of Canada. The lack of enthusiasm for the war among certain elements of English-speaking Canada was generally overlooked, but it was there, including men like Halcrow and Kerr.

As members of organized labour, they objected to the profiteering taking place on a massive scale by Canada's industrialists, much of it on the backs of unorganized labour. Munitions factories with fat government contracts were piling up enormous profits, yet in many factories their workers were among the poorest paid in the country, often earning less than twenty cents an hour.

Halcrow was an active member of the Independent Labour Party and for eight years had acted as its president. The party's platform seems moderate by today's standards, but in the early years of the century the professional and entrepreneurial classes regarded its policies as dangerously socialistic. Among the party's more objectionable planks were its call for an eight-hour day, a minimum wage, pensions for widows with children, unemployment insurance, and public ownership of utilities.

The party elected its first member to the Ontario legislature in the election of 1906 when Allan Studholme won the riding of Hamilton East. Two years later, George Halcrow joined the campaign committee of the fledgling party. Heavily committed to the cause of labour and political action, for the next two decades Halcrow was a tireless volunteer party worker in both provincial and federal elections.

A few months after the outbreak of World War I, Halcrow presided over a meeting on York Street which selected Walter Rollo to contest the riding of West Hamilton in an upcoming by-election. Rollo criticized the contractor who was building the Royal Connaught Hotel, pointing out that he was only paying his construction labourers fifteen cents an hour. Despite their appeal to the Empire and patriotism, the Conservatives only managed to defeat Rollo by the slimmest of margins.

In the summer of 1916, the employees of Davis Brothers in Hamilton walked off the job because of working conditions and low wages. For a ten-hour day, the men were earning between thirteen and sixteen dollars a week, and the women between $4.50 and $7.50 per week.

The *Hamilton Herald* had commented on the wage situation in an editorial during the early days of the war. Reflecting on a proposal for a minimum wage for city workers, it stated:

> Is twenty-two cents an hour enough to pay a robust,
> industrious man for doing hard manual work? ...
> even the steadiest worker will not be able to put in
> more than fifty hours a week. Not many of them can
> make as much as $400 a year. Can a man support a

family in decency on an income of $400 a year at the
present time? Fully a third of his income must go for
rent, leaving not much more than $250 for food, cloth-
ing, and fuel. Economize as thriftily as they may, the
breadwinner and his wife who have no more than
this sum to spend must find it hard to provide the
necessities of life for themselves and their children.

In view of the increasing cost of all commodities,
the *Herald* thinks that the proposal to raise the minimum wage to 25 cents an hour is not an unreasonable
one.[9]

The *Herald*'s comment on the increasing cost of all commodities
pointed out one of the major problems with the war for the working
man. The enormous demands for foodstuffs and munitions for
Britain's European allies, and for our own troops, pushed prices ever
upwards. Wages, especially for unorganized workers, were not keeping up. Labour demanded price controls and lobbied the federal government to that end.

In response to this pressure, and concerned that labour unrest
might spread and impair the war effort as had happened in the U.S.,
Ottawa set up a commission to inquire into complaints about labour
conditions and rates of wages at the munitions factories in Toronto
and Hamilton.

The commissioners report appeared in the spring of 1916 and recommended, among other things, that a minimum wage rate be set for
machinists of 37.5¢ per hour and for toolmakers at 42¢ per hour. The
commissioners were unable to agree on a nine-hour day.

These wages were considerably below those of plumbers who
were among the elite of the working class. By 1916, plumbers were
earning an average of five dollars a day for an eight-hour shift. If he
remained healthy and able to work fifty weeks a year, a plumber
could earn upwards of fifteen hundred dollars a year.[10]

This was the atmosphere during the years George Halcrow
served as an alderman at City Hall. He was able to build strong support with Hamilton's working classes by speaking convincingly on
matters which the city could control. He helped to gain city workers
a minimum wage of twenty-five cents an hour, and later had this
raised to thirty cents when prices rose. When the province's bakers
appeared to be acting in concert to raise the price of bread from seven
to eight cents a loaf, Halcrow and his fellow labour aldermen were

able to get a resolution through council in favour of establishing a city-owned bakery.[11]

As long as he was fighting against the capitalists and for the working man, George Halcrow was in no danger of losing his support in Hamilton's working-class north end. He had less success when he moved onto the larger federal stage and opposed the growing movement for the conscription of young men into the army. The soldiers overseas were suffering horrific losses and the conflict showed no signs of an early end. The families of these men were demanding that the "slackers" – healthy young men not already serving – should be forced to go into the army to support those serving at the front. Anti-Quebec feeling, resulting from their lack of commitment to the war effort, added racism to the strained relations between those groups clamouring for conscription and those, English and French, who were opposed to it.

The Independent Labour Party called for the conscription of wealth before the conscription of men. It wanted price controls and a corporate tax on war profits. In the federal election of 1917, George Halcrow ran in Hamilton East for the Independent Labour Party. His opponent was Major-General S.C. Mewburn, KC, minister of militia and defense. Much of the press, fraternal organizations, churches, and the financial establishment were ranged against anyone opposing conscription. The upstart Halcrow was thoroughly beaten.[12]

He had been defeated on the federal level, but he was still a force in City Hall affairs. He was very popular with his working-class constituents not only for his championing of their wage demands, but also for his opposition to the Ontario Temperance Act. The act put severe restrictions on the drinking of alcoholic beverages in Ontario. For the amoral and opportunistic, it provided an opportunity to make easy money as a smuggler or bootlegger. With all its contradictions and loopholes, the OTA laid the basis for the creation of some of Canada's wealthiest families. Both Ben Kerr and George Halcrow, old friends from their days in the union movement, were opposed to the Ontario Temperance Act. Kerr would profit from the Prohibition movement, but Halcrow's opposition would severely damage his later career as a member of the Ontario legislature.

Five

Prohibition Comes to Ontario

George Halcrow frequently took stands which were unpopular in the province at large. His stand against conscription was his most controversial, but his opposition to Prohibition was the more damaging to his career. The movement to close the bars and ban the sale of all intoxicating liquors had been around for over fifty years. It found much of its support in the Methodist Church which was then the largest Protestant denomination in Canada. The church was particularly dominant in rural Ontario where its campaign to abolish "the demon rum" found a receptive audience amongst the hard working and thrifty farmers. Many women's organizations also worked strenuously for the prohibitionist cause, believing that drunkenness was the root cause of working-class poverty, ill health, and crime.

A casual stroll through the downtown of any Canadian community on a Saturday night could lead a disinterested observer to the same conclusions as those held by the Methodist ministers and the Women's Christian Temperance Union. Drunks, lying in the streets, alleys, and doorsteps, were a common sight. There were probably more bars per capita than at any other time in this century. Women were not allowed into these sinkholes where the predominant ambiance was the overwhelming odour of stale beer, cigar smoke, and chewing tobacco. The stand up bar was the norm and a man was judged fit to drink just so long as he could remain vertical.

The working man considered the bar to be his equivalent to the professional and businessmen's private club. It was an escape from the terrible drudgery of his work and, in some cases, of his responsibilities at home. The majority of middle-class women were in favour of banning the bar, but their influence was vitiated by their lack of the franchise.

It was the Great War that finally pushed the government of William Hearst off its waffle. Hearst and his Conservative government had been gradually tightening regulations on the drinking trade but had avoided outright prohibition. The Liberal opposition charged that the Conservatives were in the pay of the brewery and distillery interests. Although true, the hypocritical Liberals, as well as the Conservatives, sent their bagmen to collect from these very lucrative sources of campaign funds.[1]

In December of 1914, Premier Hearst had shortened the closing hours of bars across Ontario from 11 p.m. to 7 p.m. Package liquor store hours were shortened from 11 p.m. to 6 p.m. The following year, Hearst passed legislation putting the control of the liquor trade directly under a five-man Board of License Commissioners with wide powers to suspend licenses for infractions, and to regulate hours of operation in accordance with local sentiment. This was not enough for the Dominion Alliance, the WCTU, the Methodist churches, or indeed for any of the prohibitionist organizations. As Samuel Chown, general superintendent of the Methodist Church of Canada, put it: "We will have nothing to do with license ... We are out to annihilate the trade."[2]

The Prohibition movement had largely been a North American phenomena. The Brits and Europeans were more concerned with maintaining the rights of the individual. This was the position taken by many Tories and churches like the Anglican Church of Canada which cited the "principles of British liberty" as the reason for its opposition to total prohibition.

This began to change as a result of the appalling cost of the Great War both in material resources and in human lives. Young Canadian soldiers survived in sodden trenches filled with layers of rotting bodies and human excreta. They charged across fields strewn with as many as 7,000 corpses per square mile, hoping that none of the machine gun and rifle fire would end their youth in that terrible place. These conditions were hidden from the public at home by rigid government censorship, but the cost in lives could not be hidden. Canadian newspapers published a list of casualties daily. These lists often took two or three pages of print, each page consisting of eight columns, each one filled with the names of soldiers either killed, wounded, or missing in action. Anxious parents and loved ones scanned the black print daily, hoping against hope that they would not find the name of their husband or son amongst the hundreds, sometimes thousands, listed. In one twelve-hour period, Canadian troops suffered over 6,000 casualties. When the war's terrible slaughter finally ended, Canada with only one-tenth the population of the United States had lost many more men. In all, Canada put 619,635 troops into the field. Of that number, the official casualties (dead or wounded) numbered 232,494.[3]

The terrible sacrifices of the soldiers finally enabled the prohibitionists to triumph. Lord Kitchener, head of the British war effort, insisted on temperance in the British army and charged that there was a definite connection between alleged German atrocities and drunkenness in their army.[4] Responding to this change in official British attitude, many Canadian newspapers either tempered their wet sentiments or came out for Prohibition for the duration of the war. The *Toronto Star* led the fight, giving lots of space to the claims of Liberal leader, N.W. Rowell. In one of his more effective charges, Rowell claimed that the money spent each year on liquor in Canada was sufficient to equip and maintain 100,000 soldiers overseas.[5] Where another 100,000 young men could be found to sacrifice themselves in that awful conflict was not explained.

The pressure on Premier Hearst and the Conservatives continued to mount. In 1916 a special group of influential citizens was formed, calling itself the "Committee of One Hundred," with the specific purpose of getting a Prohibition law passed in Ontario. In the spring, they organized a mass march of thirty thousand people on Queen's Park where a petition was presented bearing 825,572 signatures. At that time, the entire population of Ontario was only about two-and-a-half million. It was suspected that many of the names on the petition were children, but no politician dared broach the matter.

When the Ontario legislative session began in February of 1916, two provinces had already passed Prohibition laws and six more were preparing to do so. The Ontario government introduced Bill 100 on 22 March 1916. It became known as the Ontario Temperance Act and was passed unanimously on 4 April 1916. When the vote had been taken, the members rose as one and sang, "God Save The King." There were many legislators sitting in the house that day who disagreed with the bill, but so strong was popular opinion at the time that none dared vote against it.

The new act was to come into effect at 7 p.m. on Saturday, 16 September 1916. Under its terms, no establishment could stock or sell any beverage with an alcohol content above 2.5 percent. Previously, the alcohol content of beer had been 9 percent. All bars, clubs, and wholesale liquor outlets were banned.

Under the new act a person could not have, keep, give, or consume liquor except in a private dwelling house. The act did not prohibit the manufacture of liquor by licensed companies, nor did it prohibit the importation or exportation of liquor. These are federal matters beyond the powers of any province.

Newspaper writers treated the advent of Prohibition with a certain amount of sardonic humour. No doubt the press's reputation for hard drinking contributed to their outlook. It was clear from newspaper comments of the day that many reporters believed the act would be a failure and would not have much impact on drunkenness. A great deal of ink was expended commenting on the huge increase in liquor store sales the last few days before Prohibition. The *Hamilton Spectator* noted in a front-page article on the Friday before Prohibition that: "Never in the history of Hamilton have the liquor dealers done so much business as they are doing this week. Every person is stocking up in preparation for the dry spell that starts tomorrow night."

The *Toronto Star* noted the impact on the wholesale liquor stores which corresponded to present day LCBO outlets but were privately owned. The demand on these outlets was so great that by Thursday many dealers were refusing to take further orders. The *Star* observed that these outlets had attracted a new type of customer:

> Indications are that the "poor man" is going to have his store (supply). Heretofore the regular deliveries were practically all to the homes of the wealthier and well-to-do citizens. The large majority of the 11,000 new house purchasers are artisans and labourers, and the stocks laid in indicate that the "poor man" still has some surplus dollars to spend on luxuries.[6]

The impact of this new (if short lived) business must be measured against the dealers' regular customer base of 4,000 households that on the eve of Prohibition had increased almost 400 percent to 15,000 customers. For most of the dealers it was the boom before the bust. After 16 September, they either went out of business altogether or switched to selling something else.

But there were holes in the OTA and they were quickly exploited by the more resourceful retail agents. For example, Harry and Herb Hatch, the owners of a liquor store in Oshawa, moved to Montreal where they set up a mail order liquor business. Ads were placed in Ontario papers advising their customers that it was only necessary to send in their order along with a money order in the correct amount, and the liquor would be shipped directly to their home. As 16 September approached, ads began appearing in the various newspapers across Ontario advising nervous drinkers as to how they could continue to procure their favourite grog. Labatt's ran several large ads in selected newspapers across the province with this message:

Announcement
the many users of our celebrated products will be pleased to know we will continue to brew Labatt's (London) India Pale and Extra Stock Ales, XXX Stout and Canada First Lager, the superior qualities of which are well known.

Arrangements
to comply with the Ontario Temperance Act are now being made whereby those desirous of obtaining the famous old Labatt products can do so without inconvenience or delay.

Wines and Liquors
Mail Order Department
In addition to our brewing business we wish to announce that we will continue to be dealers in and carry a complete supply of wines and liquors at our warehouse.

Labatt's differed from most of the manufacturers in Ontario in that it opened an office in Hull rather than in Montreal. Moreover, Labatt's operated its mail order office with its own employees, whereas many manufacturers appointed independent agents to handle the retail part of their business.

Although not very efficient, the system worked simply enough. The Ontario customer sent his money to the agent's office in Montreal, and the agent shipped out the order from his Montreal or Hull warehouse. Some manufacturers did not even bother with this façade and simply filled the order directly from their Ontario warehouse.

Prohibition was ushered into Ontario rather more meekly than most observers had expected. In Hamilton, there were only eight arrests for drunkenness on the Saturday night of 16 September, as compared to twenty-two the previous Saturday night.

For the prohibitionists the "golden age" had arrived and the lack of activity in the police courts across the province supported this belief. During the first week of Prohibition, the Hamilton court did not have a single case of drunkenness to deal with. It was not until October 2, that Police Magistrate Jeffs had to deal with such a charge. In the early hours of Sunday morning, the defendant, William Roone, had narrowly escaped death while dancing a jig in front of a Barton streetcar. Roone's defense, that he was not inebriated but merely suffering the effects of over work, did not convince the crusty Magistrate. The miscreant was fined ten dollars. But Roone's case was fast becoming the exception across Ontario. Contrary to popular myth, in those countries in which it was tried, Prohibition resulted in a dramatic decrease in drunkenness.

The OTA caused a new type of watering hole to spring up across Ontario. They were known as "standard hotels," and were licensed under more stringent regulations than had applied to the old bars. They could serve the 2.5 percent beers, but were required to provide meals, clear and cold drinking water, conveniently located for their customers, and modern bath and lavatory facilities for both sexes. Some of the old bars and hotels were turned down when they applied for these licenses, but about 75 percent were able to qualify. In Ottawa, thirty hotels received the new licenses, ten failed to qualify, and four went out of business voluntarily. In Hamilton, out of fifty-three taverns closed down by Prohibition, thirty-eight reopened as "standard hotels."

A few of the old-style hoteliers reacted predictably, stating that they would rather go out of business than be dictated to by government. Others showed more initiative. At the Windsor Hotel on Bay Street in Toronto, the proprietor, "Chuck" Jackman, opened on Sunday, selling the near-beer and doing a good business. He credited his success to the novelty of being open on the Sabbath, no other hotel or restaurant being open in Toronto on that day! Jackman had been shrewd enough to read the new regulations and spot this opening. In the Ontario of that time, the Lord's Day Alliance Act prohibited most activities other than attendance at church. In another downtown Toronto hotel, the proprietor tried the novel idea of having barmaids replace bartenders. The young ladies were dressed in white caps, black dresses, and white aprons. The success of these innovations was temporary, business in the hotels quickly declined to the point that, by late September, fully two-thirds of Ontario's bartenders had been laid off. On 28 September, the editor of the *Hamilton Spectator* noted wryly that "if the hotelmen are doing such a poor business, then our temperance friends cannot be taking much of their own medicine."

The dramatic decline in sales resulted in many of the hotels going on the auction block. Usually the owner of the business simply hired an auctioneer to sell off the hotel's chattels. If he owned the building he would attempt to convert it to some other purpose. But the breweries and distilleries had much larger capital investments. Not all of them were prepared to quietly accept what some regarded as outright theft. The government had destroyed their business without compensation. Some of the breweries began to quietly manufacture the old 9 percent beer which they then sold illegally to the new standard hotels. The proprietor would install a special line to his draught taps and, when no inspectors were around, would sell the "real thing." This strategy lured many of the old customers back. A great deal of corruption resulted. Poorly paid license inspectors were often "bought off" by the breweries and by the hotel owners.

The poorer rural areas had a tradition of making their own "swamp whisky," usually in a homemade still, hidden out back in the woods. There was an expansion of this activity as experienced "shiners" found their product in demand by friends and neighbours.[7] In Brighton, Ontario Provincial Police Officers arrested Isaac Allcorn and seized his still, his horse, and his wagon. Allcorn was fined $800, and sentenced to seven months in jail. But, like many of these entrepreneurs, after his release, Allcorn went right back into the business. A federal government report revealed, that in the first ten months of 1919, eighty-five stills had been seized in Canada, compared with just twenty-four during the previous year, and none in each of the years previous to that.[8] In a time of economic recession, swamp whisky and bootlegging were growth industries. Taking advantage of the opportunities offered by this new industry, a few previously obscure individuals were able to rise to great power and wealth.

Six

Piano Player to Rumrunner

During the war, Ben Kerr was employed as a plumber by Bloom and Brittain. They had the contract to install the plumbing in the new, 250-room luxury hotel, the Royal Connaught. After two years of construction, it was completed in June of 1916. It quickly became the focal point of Hamilton's business and professional elites, sponsoring many fine balls and entertainments. The Royal Connaught's predominance amongst the "carriage class" is indicated by the range of entertainment offered by it over the 1917 holiday season. Attendance at these events was confirmation of one's social standing in the community.

The plumber, Ben Kerr, had helped to build the Royal Connaught, but "Bensley" Kerr, pianist, was part of the entertainment, intriguing the elegant ladies with his brooding charm and playful rendering of the "Golliwogs' Cakewalk." This was probably his last stint as a paid entertainer. Nor did he continue to work for Bloom and Brittain. After the completion of the Royal Connaught, he devoted his energies to his boat storage and rental business and, for the first time, to the building of speedboats. He had acquired the Red Wing marine-engine franchise and planned to obtain orders for power boats. His friend and business colleague, Jack Morris, would construct the hulls and decks, while Kerr Marine did the mechanical installations, including motor, steering, drive shaft, propeller, and transmission.

Following the end of the war in November of 1918, the business classes, who had grown rich supplying the war effort, helped drive a boom in the pleasure boat industry. Jack Morris advised a reporter with the *Hamilton Spectator* that he had done more work in the first six months of 1919 than in the previous three years.[1] But the boom did not last and by the middle of 1920 the country was in a full-blown recession.

It took decades for boat builders to acquire their reputations and, while many of the established Hamilton boat builders were busy, Kerr Marine was not. Ben found himself in difficult financial circumstances. He continued to take on plumbing jobs when he could get them, but the post-war recession was hard on the building industry, and the skilled trades were especially hard hit. In the midst of this recession, one industry was flourishing. Prohibition had helped to create a new class of entrepreneur, the bootlegger and the rumrunner. Many former ne'er-do-wells could not resist flaunting their new found prosperity, driving expensive cars, puffing expansively on Cuban cigars, and ordering champagne for their newly acquired "lady" friends.

The most prominent of this new class of entrepreneurs was Rocco Perri who, by the early 1920s, controlled the distribution of liquor in Hamilton, Brantford, Guelph, and all points in between. The swarthy little Italian was well on his way to becoming Canada's Al Capone. In addition to bootlegging and rumrunning, he was also deeply involved in prostitution and gambling.

Rocco was always on the move. He had contacts everywhere. It is likely that he met Ben Kerr at Jim Thompson's boat house, a popular spot with the sailing crowd. Old timers from the wharf area remember the two men being there and speaking to each other in a friendly fashion.[2] Kerr advertised "ALL NIGHT SERVICE FAST MOTOR BOAT FOR HIRE," and it is probable that the Perri gang were among his customers.[3] Rocco got his liquor from many sources and by various forms of transportation, but he was known to hire boats and likely began this practice after 1 April 1918. On that date the federal government employed the Emergency War Measures Act to stop the manufacture, movement, export or import of spirituous liquors in Canada for the duration of the war. All across the country, old and well established breweries and distilleries quietly closed their doors and laid off their employees. As the United States did not yet have prohibition, a flourishing smuggling traffic was soon under way, bringing American liquor into Canada.

Kerr was an ambitious, hard-driving man whose hard work and talents had not paid off. Moreover, some of his associates and relatives were doing extremely well. His neighbour and friend, George Halcrow, had led the polls in the 1919 election for the Hamilton Board of Control, and seemed well launched on a promising political career. In spite of the recession, Kerr's friend, Jack Morris, was doing well in the boat building business. His neighbour to the west on Bay Street was another boat builder, George Askew. Askew's reputation was well established and he too was doing a thriving business. Kerr did not have an established reputation as a boat builder, and he was not a good salesman. As a result his foray into boat building was a failure. He later told his friend Wes Thomas that "after the War, my family and I were nearly starving."[4]

Ben's lack of success was in sharp contrast to the career of his older brother. George Robert Kerr was just two years older than Ben but, by 1919, had been appointed treasurer of Canadian Westinghouse, had served as president of the Hamilton Chamber of Commerce, and was a member of both the Dominion and Ontario Legislative Committees for the Canadian Manufacturer's Association. He belonged to both the Burlington and the Hamilton Golf and Country Clubs, the Rotary Club, the Hamilton Club, and the Canadian Club. Ben belonged to none of these and knew his chances of being invited to join were zero.

All of these factors probably influenced Ben Kerr to enter into the business of rumrunning. He had the knowledge of the lake and he had the boats. For some years, he had owned a twenty-eight-foot cruiser and, in 1919, he ordered a thirty-two-footer from Jack Morris. This boat was delivered in April of 1920, which is when the navigation season on Lake Ontario begins.[5] Kerr would have been able to install the motor and other hardware and begin rumrunning by late April or early May of 1920. In August of that year, Ben Kerr was able to pay off the mortgage on his boat storage property, indicating that he had been rumrunning for at least a few months prior to August.

American Prohibition came into effect on 16 January 1920. As Ottawa's wartime ban on the liquor business had recently expired, the Canadian breweries and distilleries were getting back into production just as the American industry was shutting down. Within two weeks of the start of American Prohibition, Canadian liquor and beer was flowing across the border into the United States.

American prohibition differed fundamentally from that in Canada. In Canada, the various provinces simply passed provincial laws bringing it about. As a consequence, the law in each province was different. Under the BNA Act, provincial powers to pass laws are restricted to those powers granted them under the Act. Thus, the provinces cannot prevent the manufacture of beer or liquor, nor can they regulate its importation or export. These limitations on provincial power meant that in Canada it was perfectly legal both to manufacture spirits and to export the product to the United States. From the American point of view, this activity was illegal but, as a Canadian judge observed, "there is no burden cast upon us to enforce the laws of the United States."[6]

In order to bring about an effective and total prohibition, the Americans had gone through the time consuming process of amending their constitution. This requires a two-thirds majority vote in both the Senate and in the House of Representatives. It then requires the approval of three-quarters of the state legislatures. When all of this has been accomplished, the president can then sign the act into law. Once the constitution has been amended, it requires another amendment to the constitution (the whole process all over again) to get rid of it.

On 14 January 1919, Nebraska became the thirty-sixth state to ratify the Eighteenth Amendment. As there were then only forty-eight states in the union, the federal government had the approval of the required number of states. A year from that date (16 January 1920) the Eighteenth Amendment would come into effect and America would become legally dry. It would be illegal to transport, sell, buy, or manufacture any spirituous liquor with an alcohol content above 0.5 percent.

The enormous effort required to bring about Prohibition left its proponents drained. After more than fifty years of struggle, the prohibitionists had finally achieved their goal. Not surprisingly, many seemed to think that having won the battle no further effort was necessary – the populace would simply obey the law. These expectations proved to be hopelessly optimistic.

The Volstead Act set up the machinery to enforce the Eighteenth Amendment. The act did not make it a criminal offence to break the law, instead it would be treated as a misdemeanour, similar to a highway traffic violation. Nor was any special police force set up at the start of Prohibition. Those in authority clearly had no idea as to the extent of the problem they were facing. This attitude was frequently shared by both newspaper editors and law enforcement officials. Col. Daniel L. Porter, supervisor of internal revenue agents, confidently predicted that, "New York State is going to be as dry as the Sahara."[7] This complacency created an ideal situation for those determined to profit from Prohibition.

Faced with the loss of their livelihood, many of the men who had owned bars and hotels continued on much as before. They sold low-alcohol beer or turned their establishments into restaurants or candy stores. This was usually just a front. Their real business was selling hard liquor and high-alcohol beer, often with the cooperation of local law enforcement agencies.

When Kerr began smuggling loads of Canadian beer and liquor into the U.S., there were only *sixteen* state troopers to patrol the entire border of northern New York State. Local police forces were poorly equipped, lacking even radio communication and possessing only limited firepower. None of these enforcement agencies had boats. The United States Coast Guard was primarily a rescue service. The service had lifeboats, some of which had outboard motors, but its members were not equipped or trained to chase smugglers. As was the case with cigarette smugglers in recent years, the main worry for smugglers was not the law but other smugglers.

Kerr's testimony before the Royal Commission on Customs and Excise in 1927, makes it clear that his early source of supply for hard liquor was the Corby's Distillery, north of Belleville.

Corby's was part of the Canadian Industrial Alcohol group which controlled Consolidated Distilleries of Montreal and ran five distilleries across the country. The Corby's plant was the largest in the group and was strategically located near the Bay of Quinte and Lake Ontario. Gooderham and Worts was closer to the lake, but the aristocratic Gooderham family had decided not to sully its reputation in the now discredited booze business. As a result, when the federal government lifted its wartime closure, they did not reopen their plant near Toronto's waterfront. Gooderham and Worts was quietly put up for sale. For the first three years of Prohibition, Corby's was the only operating distillery located on or near Lake Ontario.

It did not take long for a system to evolve which would meet the technical requirements of Canadian law and provide a cover for the Americans buying Canadian whisky. Normally, the American distributor (bootlegger) would travel to the Corby's head offices at 1201 Sherbrooke Street West in Montreal. He would meet with Harry Clifford Hatch, the general manager, and establish his credentials, usually by depositing a sufficient sum of money with Hatch to establish his financial reliability and ensure delivery of future orders. Twenty thousand dollars was considered adequate.[8] Many of these "bootleggers" were men who had been wholesale liquor distributors before Prohibition. As they did not want anything on paper which could be used against them in an American court of law, they set up dummy companies with head offices in Mexico or Cuba. The orders they sent to Corby's were ostensibly from these dummy companies for delivery to Cuba or Mexico or some other country where the importation of liquor was legal. Once these arrangements were completed, the bootlegger could phone in his orders, specifying who the carrier was to be. If Kerr was the carrier, he would take his boat to Belleville where he would be met by the shipper from Corby's, a genial Irish Canadian named Jimmy Boyle. Ben would be given a B-13 customs form, which showed the amount and value of the shipment as well as its destination, and the name of the boat. He would sign as the boat's captain, confirming that the goods and destination were as set out in the form. A truck from Corby's plant north of Belleville would take the load down to the government docks where a customs officer would sign the four-part form: two copies for Canada Customs, one for Kerr, and one to the shipper from Corby's. A crew of labourers from Corby's would then load the wooden boxes of whisky onto Kerr's cruiser. Kerr kept a sharp eye on them, insisting that they treat his mahogany trimmed boat with great care. Years later, these men remember him as very particular and demanding.

Before heading out onto the lake, Kerr shook hands with J.W. Dulmage, the outside customs officer, thanking him for his assistance and leaving the latter ten dollars richer. Tipping the outside inspectors soon became standard practice with rumrunners. Some inspectors became so prosperous they bought into the business, even going so far as to purchase an interest in some of the rum boats.

Under Canadian law these transactions were technically legal. By completing the B-13's, Corby's was keeping to the letter, if not the intent, of the law. By stating that the goods were for export to a foreign country, Corby's was able to avoid paying both the sales and excise taxes. But the intent of the law was not honoured. Many of the "export boats" were under thirty feet in length, clearly too small to navigate the Atlantic. The fact that some of these boats would be back in Belleville the next day made it even clearer that their real destination had not been Cuba or Mexico, but the United States or perhaps even Ontario. The charade was further compounded by the tendency of the carriers to use an alias when signing the B-13. Ben Kerr usually signed as "John Brown."

Canadian hard liquor was in such great demand in major U.S. cities for the first several years of Prohibition that Canadian distilleries lacked the capacity to meet that demand. It was therefore more economical for them to fill the large orders which came in from the big outfits in Boston and New York than to fill the orders coming in from cities in northern New York such as Rochester and Buffalo. New York, Boston, and the American east coast was supplied by large ships, most of them chartered out of Nova Scotia, each ship taking many thousands of cases.

The shortage of whisky for lake smugglers meant that for the first four years of Prohibition men like Kerr and Perri had to rely on beer and ale for the bulk of their export business. Fortunately for them, there was no shortage of supply. The numbers varied from year to year, but during the 1920s there was an average of twenty-two breweries making beer in Ontario. Most of them were brewing strong beer for the American market. Rocco Perri purchased large quantities of beer from the Grant Springs Brewery in Hamilton, the Taylor and Tate brewery in St. Catharines, and the large Kuntz Brewery in Kitchener. Kerr's business received less publicity than Rocco's, but Kerr is known to have been a customer of the Cosgrove Brewery, the Dow Brewery, and the Hamilton Brewing Association which included the Grant Springs Brewery among its members.

Both men made huge profits. By 1920, Perri had purchased a nineteen-room mansion on Bay Street South. That same year, Kerr was able to pay off the mortgage on his boat storage operation, purchase another lot on Bay Street North, and begin construction of two new houses the following year, one of which was a beautiful four-thousand-square-foot residence for his family. He and Louisa May would no longer have to live in rented quarters.

In addition to his rumrunning activities, Kerr began "short-circuiting," a practice which put him in direct competition with Perri. Short-circuiting was the business of buying liquor, ostensibly for export, and instead of taking it across the lake, bringing it back into Ontario where it would be sold by local bootleggers or hotel owners. One of Kerr's customers was William Dillon, proprietor of the Bay View Hotel at the corner of Stuart and Bay Streets. Kerr's short-circuiting operation was not large but he was encroaching on Rocco's turf. Organized criminal gangs are highly territorial. By selling beer to Hamilton hotels, Kerr was infringing on Perri's business and territory.

At the same time, Kerr was expanding his exporting business to the United States. He got rid of his earlier boats and had Morris build him larger and faster ones. By 1922, he had two boats crossing the lake regularly. One of these was a single-engine speedboat, about thirty-five feet in length, which he called the *Evelyn*. The other was a twin-engine speedboat of about the same size. These cruisers made Kerr one of the largest smugglers on Lake Ontario.

Kerr stored his two speedboats in his boat houses that were located at the bottom of the hill behind his new home at 439 Bay Street North. He hired two local men – John Elliott and John Clark – who took turns running the smaller of the two boats. They were both working for Kerr in 1924 and 1925. The smaller boat was used for shorter trips, hauling beer from Hamilton to centres near

Youngstown, New York. The lakeside town of Olcott would later become a frequent destination.

Kerr made the longer trips, operating out of Trenton and Belleville, which were conveniently close to the Corby's distillery. Corby's would haul their load, usually about a hundred cases, down to the dock, using one of their old chain-driven Kelly trucks. From there Ben would take his boat through the Murray Canal and head directly across the lake to a point near Rochester, a journey of about four hours. On days when the weather was bad, he would head in the opposite direction, going east along the Bay of Quinte, across Big Bay, past Deseronto, and then south down Long Reach past Picton, through Adolphus Reach, and out onto the lake through Prince Edward Bay. If the weather was particularly rough, he would occasionally put in at Prinyer Cove.

At that time, Reg Powers was a teenager working on his father's farm at Prinyer Cove. Reg remembers that they were all afraid of Kerr. "He carried a big revolver and we figured if he caught any of us on his boat, he'd shoot ya," recalls Powers. Kerr seldom put in at Prinyer Cove. Usually, he went directly across Prince Edward Bay past Long Point, the most southerly point of Prince Edward County, and then directly across the open water to Main Duck Island. The island is twenty-one kilometres south of the mainland, and has the advantage of being just a few minutes boat ride north of the invisible dividing line between Canada and the United States.

Claude "King" Cole, who owned the island, was a smuggler himself. He also owned the dozen unpainted wooden cottages which ran along the shoreline of Main Duck's harbour. With their usual dry humour, the fisherman who rented these shacks had dubbed the dirt path in front of their cottages "Broadway Boulevard." The "King" had the only good looking building on the "street," – a two-storey wooden structure which he used during the summer months. Directly in front of Claude Cole's summer home was a dock and storage buildings. Cole purchased the fishermen's catch and hauled it twice a week on his fifty-two-foot trawler, the C.W. Cole, to Cape Vincent, N.Y. He used his other boat, the Emily, to haul booze to Oswego and then up the New York Barge Canal to Syracuse. Rotund and jocular, Cole enjoyed a good story, and a good drink even more. Rumrunners were drawn to the island as much by Cole's personality as by the island's natural advantages to the smuggler. Lake Ontario can be particularly rough at its eastern end, and the island's harbour, facing as it does to the northeast, is a natural haven in a storm.

In the early years of Prohibition, the island became something of a wholesale depot for lake smugglers. Cole bought large quantities of liquor and beer which he stored in the stone cellar of an old house which had fallen into disrepair. Cole built a heavy wooden door to the cellar and fashioned it with wide iron bolts so that local fishermen would not be tempted to parch their thirst at his expense. He resold some of his "cellar supply" to other smugglers, and hauled the rest of it to the States himself.

Until the fall of 1924, when his father quit fishing to go into farming, Francis Welbanks spent many summers on the island. The colourful characters he met there made a deep impression on the youngster. Ben Kerr impressed him as the most dangerous of them all. In the summer of 1922, Francis witnessed a confrontation between Kerr and two other smugglers which, sixty-six years later, was still indelibly imprinted on his memory.

"Gentleman" Charlie Mills had been a stunt pilot in northern New York State before getting into the smuggling business about 1920. Mills had a large boat, the *Adele*, forty feet long with a beam of eleven feet, capable of carrying up to five hundred cases of whisky or ale. The value of such a load made the *Adele* a tempting target for hijackers. Mills hired Claude Cole's nephew, the burly "Babe" Cole to help him run the *Adele*. Charlie himself was always armed, but for added protection he hired on George Keegan from Belleville. Keegan, who survived two shipwrecks, was considered to be one of the toughest men on the lake. In later years, Keegan was hired by the notorious Jack "Legs" Diamond, a New York hoodlum who is credited with killing at least a half-dozen rival gangsters.

Kerr got involved with "Gentleman" Charlie Mills and George Keegan in the summer of 1922. Two fishermen, Bruce Lowery and Ed Bilkey, had been caught nipping some of Mill's cache of beer. Mills and Keegan had cornered the two men, and Mills was threatening to shoot them. A group of fishermen were gathered around the dock as Mills brandished his revolver, seemingly ready to shoot Lowery who he regarded as the instigator. At that point, Kerr suddenly stepped forward and wrestled the gun away from Mills. It was done so quickly that by the time Keegan moved on Kerr he was staring into the barrel of his boss's gun. Without saying a word, Kerr then emptied the bullets from the gun and handed it over to Charlie Mills. Keegan might have been a match for Kerr, but he did not challenge the bigger man. After some hesitation and muttered threats, Keegan and Mills departed.

That Keegan, considered to be one of the toughest men on the lake, did not challenge Kerr only added to the latter's reputation. The true test of that reputation would come to rest on a much more violent confrontation, one that put to use Kerr's skills as a skeet shooter, and his ability to react instinctively under fire.

Seven

"In the Event of My Death …"

The date is not known, but sometime during his first two years as a rumrunner, Ben Kerr found himself the target of hijackers. As Don Harrison, a former Trenton rumrunner, recalls the story, Kerr was delivering a load on a lonely shore east of Rochester. He had taken his speedboat into shallow water, bow facing out for a speedy exit, engines idling, and was handing bags of ale to a man in a small rowboat, other men had waded out in water up to their waists, and were carrying bags of beer back to shore when "all hell broke lose, bullets were flying everywhere."[1] Kerr grabbed a rifle and immediately began firing in the direction of the rifle flashes. The hijackers rifle fire had driven the men on shore into the woods and had scattered the men in the water in all directions, but Kerr's highly accurate return fire drove the hijackers away from the shore and gave his associates time to regroup. Kerr then took his boat out, moved about two hundred yards east of the shooting and then landed. He landed with his .45 revolver jammed in his belt, carrying his .303 rifle in one hand and his 12-gauge shotgun in the other. He was able to come up on the rear of the hijackers and, by alternately firing the different guns, create the impression that he had others with him. In the darkness and confusion the hijackers fled the scene, without managing to steal a single case.

Francis Welbanks confirmed the essential details of the story, having heard it from a friend who had been visiting relatives in New York State.[2] The incident received wide circulation on the U.S. side, but Kerr never mentioned it. He may have feared that one or more of the hijacking party received fatal wounds, and that he could be charged with manslaughter.

Two years in the smuggling business had taken him from a struggling plumber and boat storage operator to a man of property and modest wealth. In 1921, he was able to build two houses, one for his family and the other as a rental property. He also began an expansion of his boat storage units. This increase in wealth combined with the shoot-out with the American hijackers may have led to his decision to make his will. It was filed with the court in April of 1922. It is a curious document and reveals that the marriage between Ben and Louisa May was not the happy union many people assumed.

The will left Louisa the household furniture, and a one-third interest in the estate, payable in twenty annual cash instalments. This suggests that he did not have much confidence in his wife's financial judgement. There is also a certain callousness. At the time the will was filed, Louisa May was only thirty-three years old. If she was as inept with money as the will implied, then what was to happen to her after twenty years when the payments had run out?

The big house on Bay Street and Kerr Marine Garage were left to Kerr's mother. She also received the residue of the estate, from which she was to provide for Helen, the only child of Ben and Louisa.

Ben's younger brother, Albert Ernest Kerr, was appointed guardian of Helen and was to act as trustee of any property that his mother saw fit to place in trust for her. In other words, Louisa May was given only the minimum the law required, and further, the will denied her any control over the money which Ben's mother might decide to set aside for Louisa's daughter.

The will appointed two of Ben's brothers, Albert and George, as joint trustees of the estate. Albert was a witness to the will but George was not. The other witness was J.W. Dillon, son of the owner of the Bay View Hotel. Dillon's father bought beer for his hotel from Kerr.[3]

Louisa May was a quiet, gentle person who did not smoke or drive a car. She dressed fashionably but not extravagantly, and until arthritis made it impossible, was an accomplished piano player. She doted on her daughter Helen. Outside of the home and her daughter, Louisa's principal interest was the church. She attended Christ's Church Cathedral regularly, and throughout her life was active in church activities. Fondly remembered by all who knew her, she is frequently described as having been "a real lady."

Wesley Thomas was the lighthouse keeper at Main Duck Island during the Prohibition years. Ben Kerr was a frequent visitor, apparently preferring the family atmosphere of the Thomas home to the rougher atmosphere that prevailed in the fishermen's cottages. Ben confided in Wes as in few others, explaining that he got into rum-running because he had a sick wife and daughter to support. On another occasion, he spoke regretfully of not having a son. Jack Morris Jr., who worked for Kerr for three years, mentioned that "he always treated me as a son."[4]

The lack of a son, and Louisa May's closeness to their daughter, may have been responsible for some of their marriage problems, but the real source of friction probably stemmed from the fact they were two very different people. Ben loved the outdoors whereas Louisa May preferred more refined activities. A few men who knew Ben well believe he was too domineering. Her response to his strong personality may have been to retreat emotionally from him, leaving her husband confused and isolated.

Ben Kerr seems to have responded to his marital problems by working even harder at his business and getting involved with another woman. He spent more and more time in the Trenton area where he was romantically linked with a lady named Kate.

Don Harrison was frequently invited by Ben to visit him on his boat, the *Evelyn*. Harrison met Kate there on a few occasions and recalls her as tall and athletic, with long raven hair. "She was always after Ben to let her drive the boat," remembers Harrison, who was doing a little rum running at the time. Harrison recalls that it was a warm weather affair, "Ben wasn't around (Trenton) much in the winters."[5]

Despite his involvement with Kate, Ben's first love was his boats, which he insisted be treated gently by the men loading them with liquor. Bill Lynch remembers that he would give the Corby's workers a real tongue-lashing if they were the least bit rough loading his boat. This was particularly true of the *Martimas*, which was Ben's favourite. He had ordered the *Martimas* from Jack Morris in 1923. When it was finished the *Martimas* was one of the largest rumrunners on the lake, with a capacity for as many as 1,200 cases of whisky or beer in a single trip. Its hull was made of wood, but sheathed in steel, and therefore able to break through the thin ice that was so dangerous to wooden boats trying to navigate the lake in winter. When this craft was completed in early 1924, Kerr was able to operate his smuggling business year-round, crossing the lake in winter when even the Coast Guard had put their boats in dry dock.

Kerr named the boat after the first Canadian-owned racehorse to win the Futurity Stakes at Belmont.[6] It was a cabin cruiser, forty-two feet long, quite beamy with a high freeboard, and powered by two Scripps engines, giving it a maximum speed of about fifteen knots (28 km/h). On its rear deck it carried a small dory which was used to ferry loads of booze to shore while the *Martimas* stayed out in deeper water, safe from any hijackers or Prohibition agents who might be lurking nearby.

American law enforcement agencies had been pitifully weak at the start of Prohibition but had gradually been strengthened. A special Prohibition force was set up with about 200 men posted to New York State.[7] In addition, the Customs Border Patrol was strengthened and public sentiment was building to arm and equip the Coast Guard. The wholesale violation of the Volstead Act by smugglers and organized crime had caused a backlash with the many Americans who were becoming heartily sick of the violence and corruption. Somewhat belatedly, the politicians were reacting to strengthen law enforcement.

Of more concern to Canadian liquor exporters, (a description they preferred to "smuggler" or "rumrunner"), were the attempts made by the Ontario government to make their business illegal. In 1919, the Conservative government of Sir William Hearst called an election for 20 October. The election was to coincide with a referendum on the Ontario Temperance Act. By a margin of 772,041 to 365,365, the voters of Ontario came down solidly in favour of the OTA, but threw out the Hearst's government which had brought in the act in 1916. To the surprise of practically everyone, a new political movement, the United Farmers Of Ontario, won the most seats in the legislature. They were so unprepared for their victory that they had not even bothered to select a leader. Ernest C. Drury, a farmer from Simcoe County, was belatedly chosen and became Ontario's eighth premier. A staunch prohibitionist himself, Drury picked William E. Raney to fill the post of attorney general. Raney was the attorney for the Dominion Alliance, the most anti-alcohol organization in Canada. As the cabinet officer charged with the enforcement of the OTA, Raney would prove an uncompromising enemy of the liquor industry.

Prior to the election, the United Farmers had entered into a loose alliance with the Independent Labour Party. The latter had a solid base in certain urban ridings where the farmers' party had little or no appeal. The two parties were united in their mistrust of the forces of capitalism – the professional and business classes which dominated the old-line Liberal and Conservative parties.

On the question of prohibition, the two parties were divided. The Independent Labour Party believed that the working man should have his glass of beer, and viewed the OTA as class legislation. During the election campaign, the party avoided the issue of prohibition, stating simply that it would abide by the results of the referendum.

On 20 October 1919, the electors of Hamilton returned George Halcrow as member for Hamilton East and Walter Rollo, a broom maker by trade and editor of the *Labour News*, as member for Hamil-

ton West. Both men were well qualified and might expect to be promoted to cabinet. But Halcrow's more exuberant nature dashed his
hopes of being appointed to a cabinet controlled by prohibitionists.
The day after the provincial election he travelled to Toronto in his
capacity as a Hamilton controller to deal with some hydro business.
On the way home, Halcrow, and other members of the deputation,
stopped in Oakville to celebrate his election victory. The merry making attracted the attention of a police officer who found a bottle of
whisky in the trunk of their car. Halcrow and Hydro Commissioner
Gordon Nelson were arrested and pleaded guilty the next day to a
breach of the OTA. They were each fined $200 and costs.[8] When news
of the incident leaked out Halcrow's chances of making the cabinet
evaporated. Walter Rollo was appointed by Premier Drury as minister of the department of labour. Halcrow was later elected house
leader of the Independent Labour Party. It was the high point of his
career. Independent minded and outspoken, he frequently found
himself at odds with the government he was supposed to be sup-
porting. Genial and outgoing, George Halcrow found it particularly
hard to accept the policies of William E. Raney, the severe and fanatical attorney general. Raney's attempts to stamp out the liquor trade
paid small regard to the rights of property or of the individual. When
Raney introduced radical measures to stop liquor exports, Halcrow
voted against the government. Premier Drury regarded his dubious
ally as a thorn in the government's side. In an interview with the
Hamilton Spectator, Halcrow admitted that, "I was an out-and-out wet
in the legislature."[9]

In the first two years of their mandate, the government brought
in a measure which made driving while intoxicated an offense pun-
ishable by imprisonment. While Raney could not get support for an
act to make possession of alcohol within one's home illegal, he was
able to get a bill passed which stated that where a member of a household was convicted of a breach of the OTA, no liquor could be kept in
that home until a year after the conviction. Raney also brought in a
bill empowering the police and liquor officials to search private
yachts and automobiles for illegal liquor. The drys exulted, while the
Toronto Telegram dryly observed that the only means of transportation
where citizens could be free from Raney's agents were "balloons and
submarines."[10]

Raney's strongest measures against the liquor exporters were the
Sandy Act and Bill 26 which came into effect in July of 1921. George
Halcrow led nine Independent Labour members to vote against a

clause in the act which put the burden of proof upon the defendant. Like so many single-issue politicians and fanatics, Raney cared little for personal liberty when it interfered with his self-righteous cause. The combined effect of his new laws was to prevent the movement of liquor within the province. But on 10 August 1921, Magistrate Gundy of Windsor ruled that export shipments of beer and liquor to the U.S.A. were legal. Raney had overstepped the bounds of provincial powers. The Sandy Act and Bill 26 were *ultra vires* – beyond the powers of the law – and therefore not enforceable.

The attempts by Attorney General Raney to eliminate the liquor export business caused great division within the ranks of the Independent Labour Party. When the election was called in 1923, Halcrow ran as an independent because as a Labour candidate he would have been required to support the policies of the United Farmers of Ontario. He was defeated by the Conservative candidate. After four years of a righteous and fumbling farmer's government, the electors of Ontario swept the Conservatives under Howard Ferguson back into office.

George Halcrow lost his seat in the legislature just as his friend and neighbour, Ben Kerr, was enjoying his greatest success. He was now being called the "King of the Lake Ontario Rumrunners," by Prohibition enforcement agencies in the United States. The Americans were beefing up their forces and preparing for all-out war against the rumrunners. Kerr's prominence meant those forces were singling him out for capture.

He also faced danger from Rocco Perri, the Hamilton crime boss who styled himself, "King of the Bootleggers," and was reputed to have the Hamilton police, judges, and politicians in his pocket. Kerr's growing prominence was a threat not only to Perri's business, but to his reputation and prestige. A clash between the two seemed inevitable.

Eight

The Crime Boss and the Independent

It would be difficult to imagine two more different individuals than Rocco Perri and Ben Kerr. Rocco's childhood in the south of rural Italy was marred by extreme poverty and little education. Unlike Kerr, he was physically unimpressive. Although quite short, about five-feet-four, with a swarthy complexion and thick lips, Perri more than compensated for these handicaps with his ready smile and quick wit. A natty and sometimes flamboyant dresser, he often puffed on big cigars and enjoyed bantering with police and reporters. Regardless of the pressure he was under, Rocco invariably exuded charm and good spirits. It was hard not to like the little gangster.

In contrast to Perri's humble Italian origins, Kerr came from a solid middle-class Anglo-Saxon family. Standing an inch or two over six feet, his blue eyes, fair complexion, and handsome visage emphasized his respectable origins. He was often charming and gracious but, if crossed, could be volcanic and threatening. In his early years, "Bensley" Kerr often wore the wide-brimmed foppish hats favoured by artists and musicians. But in later years Ben preferred the Arundel which was similar to the popular fedora but more stylish, with a sharply turned up brim. Although he was frequently around boats and equipment, Kerr was usually an elegant dresser. In winter he wore a large coonskin coat. Like the majority of men at that time, he smoked cigarettes and occasionally a cigar.

Perri was born in the village of Plati, Italy, two days after Christmas in 1887. Plati is near the toe of the Italian boot and is about twenty kilometres inland from Calabria, a region known for its crime family, the Calabrian N'Dranghita or Honoured Society. Today, criminals from the Plati control most of the drug trade in Australia. Like hundreds of thousands before him, Rocco left his barren homeland to make his fortune in the United States. He was fifteen years old when he arrived in New York City. He probably lived in the slums of Little Italy or East Harlem. Five years later, Rocco entered Canada from White Mountain, Vermont, and settled for a few months in Montreal. He spent time in Parry Sound and Trenton, Ontario. He had been in Canada four years when he came to Toronto in 1912 and took a room in the "Ward," an area bounded on the south by Queen Street, on the north by College, on the east by Yonge, and on the west by University Avenue. This vast slum was inhabited primarily by immigrants, struggling to survive in the New World. Public health inspectors condemned the Ward's housing for overcrowding, open sewage, and a lack of indoor plumbing. In 1911, the medical officer of health condemned 108 houses as unfit for human habitation. Nevertheless, they continued to be occupied by impoverished families.

Bessie (Starkman) Tobin lived in the Ward with her two small daughters and her husband, Harry Tobin, a bakery driver. Bessie's family was Jewish and had fled Russia in order to escape the pogroms sweeping that land. Sometime in 1912, Bessie took in Rocco Perri as a boarder. Perri, who was eking out a subsistence existence as a construction worker, wooed and quickly won the vivacious Bessie. Rocco was ambitious and articulate, but his difficulty in reading and writing English, combined with his immigrant status, restricted him to the most menial of jobs. Despite Perri's seemingly poor prospects, Bessie abandoned both her husband and her two small children to live with her paramour.

Like so many ambitious immigrants, Rocco turned to crime, one of the few avenues of upward mobility open to a man in his circumstances. In 1912, Perri travelled to Elk Lake, in northern Ontario, and paid a visit to a Giuseppe Portilesi who owed Rocco fifty dollars. Perri was acting for a man in Toronto who owned a house in Elk Lake. Rocco told Portilesi that he was to burn the house down or he would be turned out of the house he was living in. Fire destroyed the house on 16 February 1912. Portilesi eventually received ten years for arson but, in an attempt to save himself, wrote a letter to the chief of the Elk Lake Police telling about Perri's role in the fire. Portilesi later denied the truth of the letter and Perri escaped prosecution. Under the name of Fred Cortelesa, Portilesi resurfaced years later as a member of the Perri gang in Hamilton.[1]

This is the first known criminal incident involving him. For the next several years, he worked as a construction labourer in the St. Catharines and Welland areas. He and Bessie were desperately poor, dressed in threadbare clothes, and with barely enough to eat. At one point Rocco was working as a construction labourer on the Welland Canal, and was so poor that he could not afford shoes.

With the outbreak of the Great War in 1914, funding for the canal was stopped and Rocco had to take part-time work in the bakery of Filippo Mascato. A secret Ontario Provincial Police report suggests the shadowy Mascato had ties to Italian crime families. It was probably through Mascato that Rocco obtained his introduction into the workings of the underworld in Canada.

By 1916, Rocco and Bessie were living in Hamilton at 157 Caroline Street North. His previous employer had closed his bakery and gone back to Italy, throwing Perri out of work. Most Italian immigrant males had gone to work for the steel mills, which, because of the war, were working around-the-clock. But Rocco was already moving into crime on a serious scale. He took a job as a part-time salesman for the Superior Macaroni Company. As the work involved travelling, it was an ideal cover for Rocco who by this time was setting up his numbers racket. He travelled in a seventy-kilometre radius from Hamilton setting up bookies, then called "handbook men," who took bets on the horse races at factories, offices, newsstands, and even made house calls at the private homes of the wealthy.

Exactly when Perri got into this business is not known, but bookmaking had enormous potential. In 1923, Ernest Hemingway reported in the *Toronto Star* that Toronto was known throughout the world as one of the biggest betting towns in North America. Hemingway estimated that, every day of the week, at least $100,000 of illegal betting took place in the city.

With the introduction of Prohibition to Ontario on 16 September 1916, Rocco and Bessie immediately broadened their criminal activities to include bootlegging. Initially, booze seems to have been just a sideline to the small-scale prostitution which they operated from their house. There were about five thousand Italians in Hamilton, most of them single men who could not afford to bring wives over from their homeland and who were not considered respectable enough for Anglo-Saxon girls to date. These men lived in crowded rooming houses and worked long and hard for wages that had not kept up with wartime inflation. Lacking the family and friendships of home, and denied the company of marriageable women, they were ready customers of cheap prostitutes. A study done by Ernest Bell on prostitution in America, concluded that there was more white-slave trafficking in Hamilton than in any other city of its size in the whole of North America.[2]

Initially, Bessie hired prostitutes to work out of her house on Caroline Street. To supplement this business, Rocco ordered booze by the case through the mails from Quebec, selling drinks to the prostitute's customers at fifty cents a shot. Bootlegging was initially just a profitable sideline to the main business of prostitution.

Late in 1917, Bessie and Rocco bought a small grocery store at 105 Hess Street North. Rocco began selling liquor across the counter of his shop. Soon, the booze business was more important than prostitution. The duo quickly became wholesalers to the many local bootleggers in Hamilton. Bessie handled the orders while Rocco made the contacts with the bootleggers and continued to expand his numbers racket by recruiting the bookmakers or handbook men. These activities were so profitable that, in 1920, Rocco and Bessie sold the grocery store and moved to a nineteen-room mansion on Bay Street South. The top floor of this three-storey building was used for a time as the communication centre for the bookmaking operation. Business was doing so well that, in the summer of 1920, they chartered a yacht to take their friends and "business associates" out on the lake so that they could party, free from the prying eyes of the police.

The advent of Prohibition in the United States opened up a huge market for bootleggers like Rocco and Bessi. Other criminals were moving into this highly profitable market and a bootleggers' war broke out in the area from Hamilton through to Niagara Falls. Before it was over, the Ontario Provincial Police had seventeen murders in which they suspected Rocco was involved or connected. He was never charged, and it is unlikely he ever killed anybody himself. That was not Rocco's style. He ordered things done and was careful to insulate himself from the deed.

By the winter of 1922, the bootleg war was over. The three Scaroni brothers, who had controlled bootlegging in Brantford and Guelph, had been murdered and their operation taken over by Perri, who somehow managed to remain friendly with the surviving widows and relatives. In the secret world of crime, his charm and shrewdness, along with Bessie's administrative skills and toughness, had made them the largest bootleggers in Ontario. By 1924, the Perris were millionaires.

Along with a fleet of trucks and automobiles used to distribute booze in Ontario, as well as run it across to the States, the Perri's now owned a cruiser, the *Atun*, capable of carrying six to seven hundred cases of liquor at a speed of twenty knots (37 km/h). They also leased boats and hired rumrunners to take their cargoes into the U.S.A.

From the beginning of American Prohibition, the Perris had purchased Canadian whisky where ever they could get it. The huge American market would take all the beverage alcohol they could supply. In 1923, Rocco purchased 2,554 bottles of whisky from the Corby's distillery north of Belleville. The load was taken to the dockside from the Corby's plant via the old Grand Trunk line (recently absorbed into the C.N.R.), and then loaded on to the thirty-three-foot cruiser, the *Hattie C.* The boat's destination was given as the United States but, on the evening of 5 October, its crew attempted to land their cargo at Ashbridge Bay at the foot of Leslie Street in Toronto. Acting on a tip from rival bootleggers, Toronto police managed to capture the boat and its crew but not before one of the smugglers, John Gogo, had been shot and killed.

Rocco Perri along with several others at the site were arrested. Never lacking in gall, Perri explained that he was there by accident and had simply given directions to strangers. The fact that some of the trucks seized at the site belonged to Bessie was not explained. Subsequent developments left no doubt that Rocco and Bessie were the buyers of the whisky.

At the time of the Gogo shooting, Harry Hatch was the general manager of Corby's and his brother, Herb, along with Larry McGuiness, were the chief sales agents. Shortly thereafter, the Hatch brothers severed their connection with Corby's and purchased the old Gooderham and Worts plant in Toronto.

In 1924 the Gooderham and Worts distillery was reopened and became a major supplier for both Ben Kerr and Rocco Perri. The Hatch brothers had had a falling out with Sir Mortimer Davis, the owner of Corby's. Harry Hatch, who had been hired by Davis as his general manager, had increased sales at Corby's from 500 to 50,000 gallons a month. When Sir Mortimer reneged on his promise to give shares in his company to the Hatch brothers, Harry Hatch went to the Gooderham brothers to see if he could buy their idle distillery. The Gooderhams were at first reluctant, not wishing to sell to that "Montreal Jew." Once they realized Hatch and Sir Mortimer were on the outs, they were more than happy to make a deal with the young and aggressive Hatch brothers. So much so that William George Gooderham, as president of the Bank of Toronto, was able to arrange a loan to facilitate the deal. On 23 December 1923, Harry Clifford Hatch and associates purchased the Gooderham plant in Toronto (just north of the present day Gardner Expressway), along with the goodwill and brand names of Canada's oldest distillery, for just $1.5 million.

It was a bargain basement price. Hatch did not have the plant in operation until April of 1924, yet within two years, Gooderham and Worts was earning a yearly profit equal to the original purchase price.[3] This was largely due to Hatch's aggressive approach to sales in both the U.S.A. and Canada. His older brother, Herb Hatch, and Larry McGuiness formed a company called Hatch and McGuiness which took orders from bootleggers such as Perri. Bessie would actually phone in the order to Hatch and McGuiness. They, in turn, phoned a telegraph office in New York State, instructing them to send a wire for the order. If Perri was going to smuggle the order back into Canada, the telegraph company would be instructed to sign the order, "J. Penna of Wilson, New York." This procedure was followed so that Gooderham and Worts could argue that they were not breaking the Ontario Temperance Act by selling in Ontario, but were shipping to the United States, which was legal. The telegraph was their proof that the order was for export. The company of Hatch and McGuiness was really just a front to preserve appearances.

The Hatch brothers had risen from lowly bartenders, but Harry Hatch was sensitive to the charge that they had engaged in any illegal activity. Herb was not so particular and, in later years, loved to regale his acquaintances with tales of the "bad old bootlegging days."

Bessie was soon placing most of her whisky orders with the ambitious Hatch brothers, perhaps because they obligingly granted her a $20,000 line of credit. Rocco would later boast to a *Toronto Star* reporter that he sometimes sold as many as a thousand cases of whisky a day.

By late 1924, the business was becoming increasingly competitive. Corby's distillery had carried out a major expansion of its production facilities, making it the largest distilling plant in the British Empire. The Bronfmans were building a large distillery in Montreal, and the Hatch brothers were preparing to expand their capacity. The increased production capacity of Canadian distillers and resulting competition made Rocco Perri a particularly important customer to Gooderham and Worts. In addition to the large orders he was giving the company to supply his own organization in Ontario, he used his U.S. connections in the Italian underworld to arrange orders for them from Dominic Sacco in Chicago, Nino Sacco in Buffalo, and Rocco Pitsimenti in N.Y.C.'s Little Italy. Naturally, Rocco got a cut on these orders.

In late November of 1924, the Perris agreed to be interviewed by Dave Rogers, a young *Toronto Star* reporter. Rogers was admitted into the Perri mansion at 166 Bay Street South to meet the impeccably dressed couple in their lavishly appointed living room. To Roger's amazement, Rocco and Bessie not only admitted that they were bootleggers, but that Rocco was known as the, "King of the Bootleggers." Perri went on to state that, "my men do not carry guns. If I find that they do, I get rid of them. It is not necessary. I provide them with high-powered cars. That is enough. If they can not run away from the police, it is their own fault. But guns make trouble. My men do not use them." Muted classical background music lent an air of unreality to an interview dealing with murders, bootlegging, and Perri's justification for breaking the law. "The law, what is the law? They don't want it in the cities. They voted against it. It is forced upon them. It is an unjust law. I have a right to violate it if I can get way with it ... I shall do it in my business until I get caught. Am I a criminal because I violate a law that the people do not want?" He then went on to state his code of honour. "I would not kill him. I would punish him. That is the law of the Italians. We do not go to the police and complain. That is useless. We take the law into our own hands. I would kill a man on a question of honour, but not if he merely informed on me. We believe we have the right to inflict our own penalties. Sometimes it is necessary to kill a man. But I have never done it, and I don't want to." Bessie Perri became involved in the interview when the matter of principles came up, stating, "you have heard that there is honour among thieves, but maybe you do not know that there is such a thing as principle among bootleggers. Yes, we admit we are bootleggers, but we do our business on the level."[4]

It was a classic newspaper scoop. "King of Bootleggers won't stand for guns," proclaimed the headline on the *Star*'s front page. Within hours the newspaper had sold out. By the end of the day a copy of the *Star* was fetching a hundred times its regular price of two cents. But admitting to being a bootlegger was not evidence of any specific crime, and to the embarrassment of the police and justice system, Rocco and Bessie could not be prosecuted.

Given the scope of their operation, it was inconceivable that the Perri organization would allow an independent to operate in the heart of their territory. Ben Kerr was an insult to Perri power and had to be dealt with. Sometime in April or May of 1925, Perri went to Gooderham and Worts for a meeting with Herb Hatch and Larry McGuiness. Among the subjects of discussion was the threat posed by Ben Kerr to Perri's business in the Hamilton area. It was agreed that Rocco would get a monopoly. If Ben Kerr wanted to buy whisky from Gooderham and Worts, he would have to buy under terms dictated by Rocco and Bessie.

What arrangements were made between the Perris and Kerr is not known, but in the fall of 1926, records turned over to the Ontario Provincial Police by the Gooderham and Worts distillery show Kerr as a regular customer. It is also known that Kerr was buying raw alcohol from Joseph Sottile of Niagara Falls, New York and smuggling it back into Canada. As Sottile was part of a larger crime organization with close connections to Perri, it is unlikely Kerr could have dealt with Sottile without Rocco's approval. Rocco was undoubtedly the go-between, setting up Kerr with Sottile as part of a deal whereby Kerr agreed not to compete with Perri's Ontario bootlegging operation, in return for the opportunity to bring American raw alcohol into Hamilton for Perri. Kerr would receive a fee for his services as a smuggler. Perri may also have provided Kerr with more American customers. No doubt the shrewd little Italian took a cut on Kerr's profits on these sales. There is documentary evidence that Kerr began delivering Canadian liquor to American bootleggers who were allied with Joseph Sottile. The deliveries were made to Olcott, New York, which is conveniently close to Hamilton. Previously, Kerr's customers were near Rochester and Oswego. Both cities are several hours farther from Hamilton by boat than is Olcott.

The extra business provided by Perri led Kerr to expand his smuggling operation. By the summer of 1925, Kerr was operating three good-sized cruisers on Lake Ontario. Kerr piloted his largest boat, the *Martimas*, and hired on John Elliott and John Clark as crew. Nothing is known about Clark, but Elliott was a Hamiltonian who kept a float plane not far from Kerr's Marine Garage. Elliott probably used the plane to monitor the movements of the Coast Guard fleet on Lake Ontario.

Aside from Clark and Elliott, Kerr had at least two other men employed to drive his smaller boats. The ubiquitous Perri probably put Kerr in contact with one of these, Alf "Gunner" Wheat, who quickly became Kerr's most courageous and trustworthy employee.

Wheat was born in Leicestershire, England on 1 October 1885, and was living in Hamilton with his wife, Rose, and their two sons when the Great War broke out in Europe. He initially joined the Imperial Yeomanry but later transferred to the Canadian Expeditionary Force, serving as a linesman with the 34th Battery where he demonstrated "remarkable devotion to duty and courage" and "great courage and resource" at St. Eloi while under "heavy hostile barrage." For this action, he was awarded the Military Medal. A few months later, at Courcelette, he distinguished himself once again, saving the life of the soldier working with him by dragging the man to safety before returning to the task of repairing the communication lines which the Germans had "under the most heavy hostile fire."[5] For this he received the Bar to the Military Medal. In between these decorations, Wheat was promoted from gunner to bombardier and then reprimanded and demoted back to gunner. Like many Canadians he was too independent for the discipline of military life. In April of 1917, Gunner Wheat joined 100,000 Canadian troops in the Dominion's greatest wartime victory, the battle of Vimy Ridge. It was here that Canada's citizen army accomplished what the British and French professionals had been unable to do. In the five days of battle, Canada's casualties numbered 10,602 of which 3,598 were fatal. Wheat was wounded on the second day of the battle, receiving shrapnel wounds to his arm, leg, and hip. He was sent to military hospital in Sharncliffe, England, and after a lengthy convalescence, was discharged and shipped back to Canada, arriving in January of 1918. Although his wounds had left him with a permanent limp, Wheat had no difficulty in finding work. Canada's factories were stretched to their capacity, supplying guns and ammunition for the war effort. He was hired on as an electrician at Dominion Foundries.

As the war drew to a close, many returning soldiers brought with them a deadly killer. By the fall of 1918, Spanish influenza was sweeping Ontario, closing schools, churches, offices, and even factories. As neither sulpha drugs nor antibiotics had yet been invented, the medical profession could do little, and suffered heavy casualties itself from the highly contagious disease. Tragically, young adults in the prime of life were particularly susceptible to the bacteria. Doctors commented that, in many families, the grandparents and young children were not affected but the parents were ill or dying. The two sons of Alf and Rose Wheat did not contract the disease, but their mother, Rose, died from it. Barely a year after returning from the war, Alf Wheat found himself a widower, working forty to fifty hours a week and attempting to take care of two young sons.

Many Canadian families were in similar circumstances. Before it was over, the Great Influenza Epidemic of 1918–19 had killed somewhere between 30,000 and 50,000 Canadians. Reliable numbers are not available, as doctors and hospitals were too overworked and short-staffed to keep accurate records.

Like Alf Wheat, Louisa Wilkinson of Hamilton lost her partner to the flu and was left with two children to support. Her position was the more difficult as job opportunities for women were limited and the pay, even for the same work, much lower. But fortune intervened, saving the dark-haired Louisa from the drudgery of doing other peoples' laundry and housework. Her husband's grave was about thirty feet from that of Rose Wheat, and eventually she and Alf Wheat met while visiting the graves of their dead spouses. According to family legend, they met when Louisa asked Alf to help her with her camera. The blond, blue-eyed Alf was smitten by the tall, dark-eyed Louisa and after a brief courtship, they were married. Eventually their children totalled seven, two from each of their first marriages and three from their union.

In 1920, Alf moved the family to a rented house at 75 Dundurn Street. The house had a garage at back which was convenient for Alf's new business, running truckloads of beer from the Kuntz brewery in Kitchener to bootleggers and rumrunners in Hamilton. Lacking much capital, Wheat had purchased an old National truck. Its solid rubber tires made for a bone-jarring ride and the single magneto-powered headlight made night driving hazardous. But Alf had an advantage over many of the rumrunners. Alec Roughhead, a Hamilton detective, was a good friend and kept Alf posted on police movements. Later, when Alf had expanded his operation by building a large garage on his property, hiring another driver, and buying two new Reo trucks, he was able to keep ahead of police raids. Detective Roughhead would tip Alf off in time for him to move the beer out of his garage to another location.[6]

Bootlegging and rum running were dangerous activities. Wheat was not a big man, fairly short and of medium build, but he was no stranger to violence and was skilled with firearms. On one occasion, he returned home in his model-T Ford, and when he did not emerge from the garage, Louisa and her son, Fred, went out and found him in the car so badly beaten they had to carry him into the house. He was in bed for a week recovering from the attack by two unknown assailants.

Like Kerr, Wheat was an independent working in Perri's territory. His son, Len, remembers that someone – his father never said who – began forcing Alf's trucks off the road and that his father finally agreed to work for the gang responsible. Perri was too shrewd to kill off tough veterans like Wheat. It was better to have them working for his organization.

It may have been the swarthy little crime boss who brought Alf Wheat and Ben Kerr together, knowing that Ben needed another driver for the new boat he had purchased. As Alf was busy running loads in his two trucks, he would be the logical person to make the short trips to Olcott, New York. The round trip, including unloading, would only take about three hours.

Jack Morris Jr., who travelled with Kerr and Wheat for three years, recalls that the two men got along well together and never argued. The little Englishman's cheery nature had a positive effect on the disposition of the sometimes choleric Kerr.

While the relationship between Perri and Kerr was no doubt profitable for both of them, given Ben's explosive personality and his unwillingness to take orders, the relationship had to be stormy. Moreover, Ben shared the traditional attitude towards women, namely that their place was in the home and that men made the major decisions. This outlook strained relations whenever Ben had to deal with the flinty Bessie.

The strained relationship between Kerr and Perri is made clear by an OPP undercover report on the Gooderham and Worts distillery. Noting Perri's control over Hamilton, and Kerr's reputed threat as a competitor, the agent reported that on one occasion when Kerr was taking a delivery, he was warned by an employee of the distillery not to land his cargo on the Canadian side of the border. "Tell them to go to hell," barked Kerr, "they know where I am going to land." He then went on to state that arrangements had been worked out personally between himself and Larry McGuiness. The agent went on to write, "I afterwards understood that Kerr was bucking the Perri business and naturally the distillery wanted to protect Perri, she [clearly he is referring to Bessie] being one of their biggest buyers."[7]

The uneasy alliance between Kerr and Perri held together for a while largely because of financial advantage, but also in part because they shared an outside enemy. By 1925 the United States Coast Guard had equipped its officers and men with fast, well-armed patrol boats and was driving many rumrunners into safer lines of work. Moreover, the OPP had expanded and was becoming a threat to those smugglers bringing their cargoes back to Ontario. However prickly Kerr was to deal with, Rocco Perri needed him and his boats.

Kerr kept his agreement with Perri secret. Old timers who knew both men did not think they were connected in any way. But documents seized by the OPP and U.S. officials reveal that Kerr worked with the Perri mob. In the midst of this extension into activities involving organized crime, Kerr was developing the image of a substantial and respectable business and sportsman. In 1924, he began a major expansion of his boat repair and storage facility on Bay Street

North. When it was finished, he was one of the largest marine operators in the Hamilton-Burlington area.

In March of 1925, a reporter from the Hamilton *Herald* made a tour of the recently completed expansion of Kerr's Marine Garage and wrote a glowing report on the new facility noting that:

> In this group of buildings ... are accommodations for more boats than the *Herald* man ever saw at one time around Hamilton. Power boats up to 60 feet can be floated right inside, and if not over 20 tons weight can be raised up bodily for winter storage or for temporary repairs. There are seven hundred feet of buildings, separated into seventy-five parts, with fire-proof iron walls, each compartment being allotted to a boat owner ... there are rest rooms, wash rooms, liberal boat landings, and a forty foot veranda, twenty feet above the water and all under roof ... there are marine railway, paint shop, gasoline storage, stock rooms, and everything necessary for motor boats, just as one would expect to find in a car garage ... (parking) space for twenty cars is provided on the premises.[8]

What the reporter didn't know was that the new garage contained three secret doors which led into rooms where Kerr could store contraband spirits smuggled in from Niagara Falls.

In addition to his now flourishing boat storage and repair business, Ben Kerr had become involved in sponsoring a sports team. Kelly Thompson, the team's manager, had come to him asking for financial support for the Pals hockey team. The players were mostly young men in their twenties who owned small boats and rented lockers from Jim Thompson's Boat Works. Kerr was enjoying his financial success and readily agreed to sponsor the team. Once he got involved, Ben never missed a game. The industrial league was very popular in Hamilton, often selling out the old Barton Street Arena. Kerr would cheer the players on at the arena, and then have them back to his house after the games, supplying free beer. This was greatly appreciated by the players as the Ontario Temperance Act was still in effect. As Kelly, who was a teetotaller, remembers it, "I think Ben had the best fun he ever had in his life ... I never heard of him doing anything where he had any fun, other than the team."[9]

It was a high point in Kerr's life. He was helping to put his younger brother, Albert Ernest, through engineering at university. In addition, he had built a studio in his big house on Bay Street for his daughter, Helen, who was developing into an accomplished dancer. Louisa May Kerr spent many hours playing the piano while her daughter practised her dance routines. Moreover, Ben's sponsorship of the Pals hockey team, combined with the enlarged and modernized facilities of Kerr Marine Garage, had earned him a prominence in the business and sporting community. This respectability would be destroyed if his association with Rocco Perri became public knowledge.

Ben Kerr's connection with Rocco Perri while profitable, was potentially destructive not only to his reputation but also to his smuggling business. By granting an interview to Dave Rogers of the *Star*, Rocco and Bessie had not only grabbed the headlines, they had also grabbed the attention of law enforcement agencies in both Ottawa and Toronto. The RCMP began an undercover action on Perri, while the OPP increased its attempts to put the Italian crime boss behind bars. By preening in public, the Perris had embarrassed both law enforcement agencies and the judicial system itself. Henceforward, the arrest and prosecution of the Perris became a priority for both the provincial and federal governments.

Nine

Turning the Tide
against the Law Breakers

When the U.S. Congress brought in Prohibition with the passage of the Eighteenth Amendment, a great many prohibitionists believed that they had slain the liquor dragon. That large numbers of the populace would flout the sacred Constitution was not anticipated. Within weeks after the passage of Prohibition, the United States was awash in illegal alcohol. Prohibitionists across the land began to mobilize to pressure Congress into taking whatever steps were necessary to end the epidemic of bootlegging and rumrunning. In an era when the best government was considered to be the least government, especially when government meant the spending of taxpayers' money, any attempt to stop smuggling by spending money was regarded with deep suspicion. Nevertheless, the wholesale flouting of the Constitution was so anathema to ordinary Americans that Congress finally found the nerve to bring in a bill to appropriate the funds needed to strengthen the Coast Guard. In the meantime, the president had been negotiating with the U.K. (Canada did not then control its own foreign affairs) for an agreement which would make it illegal for Canadians to export liquor to the United States. England's trade interests disposed them to cooperate with the Americans, but Canada's assistance to the mother country during the Great War prevented England from selling out the colony's interests totally. In 1924, both of these developments came together. After that the tide began to turn slightly in favour of the enforcement agencies and against the smugglers.

In that year, the Canadian and American governments signed a convention which was to come into effect on 17 July 1925. The United States had pushed hard for the right to have "liquor exporters" extradited, but Canada refused on the grounds that the offense had to be a crime on both sides of the border. If it was not an offense in Canada, then the Canadian government would not cooperate in any extradition proceedings.

Britain and Canada did agree that Canada's customs service would notify American authorities of any boat clearing a Canadian port with a load of liquor destined for the United States. The Americans would be notified as to the name of the boat, its cargo, date cleared, and destination. Initially, this appeared to pose some danger to the smugglers because they could expect a warm reception from U.S. law enforcement officers when they tried to land. The smugglers adopted several tactics to minimize the effects of this convention. After clearing from Belleville with a load of whisky, or from Deseronto with a load of beer, rumrunners often put in at Main Duck Island for a few days, hoping that after a day or two the Coast Guard and U.S. Border Patrol would assume they had missed the smuggler and would relax their vigilance.

Another tactic was to give a false destination. The smuggler might give Oswego as his destination but land instead near Rochester. It was also common for the smuggler to change the name of his boat en route. The names of some boats were painted on a board which slid into groves nailed to the bow of the boat. Once out of port, the board would be pulled out and a new board and name inserted into the grooves.

Often, the Canadian Customs officers looked the other way and the smuggler simply used fictitious information when filling in the B-13, giving a false name for the boat, himself, and his destination. Before leaving port, the rumrunner would make a "donation" to the custom officers' benevolent fund.

The governments of Ontario and the U.S. passed other legislation to discourage the smugglers. By mid-1924, both governments had passed laws enabling them to seize the boats, the automobiles, and the trucks, on which contraband liquor was found. Provision was made by the American government for the Coast Guard to second any seized ships for use as rum chasers. In this manner, the Coast Guard was able to gradually build up a large and versatile fleet capable of chasing and catching all but the fastest rum ships.

In Ontario the police were getting more efficient at catching those rumrunners who were smuggling their loads back into the province instead of taking them to the United States. The practice of short-circuiting was carried out on a large scale by Perri and others. These large-scale operators came to regard the loss of the occasional load to the police as just part of the cost of doing business.

The short-circuiters had little difficulty avoiding small-town police forces, most of which consisted of a town constable with little more than a billy and a whistle for equipment. Much more effective was the OPP which had a motorcycle unit and at least one squad car in each division. In its annual report for 1924, the force reported that it had seized 4,444 cases and 29,950 gallons of beer, 3,665 cases of whisky, and 3,899 gallons of alcohol. In the first year of the new legislation permitting the force to seize autos, it seized and confiscated forty-seven. The OPP laid a total of 4,187 charges under the OTA, and obtained 3,442 convictions. Altogether an excellent record for a police force numbering only 196 officers in all ranks.[1]

In the larger metropolitan centres, the police were able to make some inroads on the smugglers. The most sensational of these was the killing of John Gogo, the wounding of his uncle, James Gogo, and the seizure of the rumrunner, *Hattie C*, along with 110 cases of Corby's whisky. The accomplishment was marred by the subsequent trial of the four Toronto policemen for manslaughter which ended in a hung jury. While the policemen got off, the trial made it clear that they could not shoot at smugglers simply because they were trying to escape. They could shoot only if their own lives or that of innocent civilians were in danger.

In spite of this restriction on their methods, Toronto police made some inroads against smugglers, most notably on those using motor vehicles. One of their more sensational captures occurred in November of 1923, just a month after the Gogo shooting. It began when officer Bill Ward and his partner, Norm Shuttleworth, noticed a truck leaving the Dominion Brewery on Queen Street. They stopped the vehicle on Parliament Street north of Dundas Street, seized 940 bottles of beer and arrested the driver. A large touring car and its five occupants, which had been escorting the truck, sped north on Parliament Street at speeds of up to 100 kilometres per hour, with Ward in hot pursuit. The chase took detective Ward west along Gerrard Street to Jarvis Street where the miscreants turned north. Ward followed, steering his 1923 squad car with one hand and working his siren with the other. The fleeing touring car crashed into a truck at the corner of Isabelle Street but continued weaving wildly through heavy traffic until thirty kilometres later the vehicle crashed through an iron fence as the driver tried to navigate a lane way at high speed on Major Street. The chase had covered more than thirty kilometres, and two motorcycle policeman, who had been chasing the vehicle, were shaken off, but detective Ward was not. He pursued the five fleeing men on foot and captured two of them.[2]

The ingenuity of the smugglers was often matched by excellent detective work. Patrol Sergeant Francis and Constable Crowson were not fooled by a shipment of "formaldehyde and soda" sent in barrels to a Toronto chemical company on the CNR. They investigated and found the barrels contained 719 bottles of whisky. That same day the officers examined another freight car in the Cherry Street yards and seized another 768 bottles.[3]

On 12 May 1924, Canada Customs ruled that liquor could not be shipped on trains if destined for the United States. Naturally the smugglers tried to side-step the ruling but smuggling on freight trains declined. Power boats, automobiles, and trucks remained the major means of transport for the smugglers.

While the police forces of Ontario had some success against those smugglers who brought booze back into the province, they played no role in preventing rumrunning into the United States. This was strictly an American problem. State police, Customs Border Patrol, Prohibition agents, and local police, all played some role in enforcing the Volstead Act. Unfortunately, they were poorly paid, and especially the newly created Prohibition Agency, susceptible to corruption by the bootleggers who had lots of money to spread around. During the years of its existence fully one quarter of the men recruited by the force were dismissed for larceny. On a salary of just $2,000 a year, some agents somehow managed to arrive for work in chauffeured limousines. Despite the corruption, in 1923 alone the Prohibition Agency seized 134 rumrunning vessels and 3,977 automobiles. Although eleven agents were killed, and twenty-eight wounded or injured, the number of seizures increased steadily for several years thereafter.[4]

But the Prohibition agents did not seriously threaten the operations of smugglers like Kerr. The various American police forces were not equipped to apprehend law breakers on the water. Unfortunately for Kerr and lake smugglers generally, their success finally forced Congress to spend the money needed to make the Coast Guard an effective weapon in the war against the smugglers.

In the spring of 1924, Congress approved the expenditure of some $14 million with the objective of turning the Coast Guard from a life-saving service into an anti-smuggling force. A portion of the money was to be spent building vessels suitable for patrolling the Great Lakes and the inshore waters of the Atlantic and Pacific coasts. It was also used to improve shore facilities. A machine shop and a radio station were to be built at Buffalo, specifically to service and communicate with the patrol ships in their battle against the smugglers. Radio was a new technology, but some of the more sophisticated smugglers were already using it. Ben Kerr was one of them.

Two classes of boats were built. The larger was a seventy-five-foot patrol boat, or "six-bitter." Manned by a crew of eight, and powered by twin 200 horsepower Stirling six-cylinder gasoline engines, these vessels were capable of a speed of fifteen to sixteen knots (30 km/h). Their armament consisted of a .30-calibre machine gun, small arms, and a one-pound cannon mounted on the fore-deck. Although not as fast as some of the rumrunners, the six bit-ter's cannon, with an accurate range of two miles, made it particu-larly effective against smugglers on the Great Lakes.

The six-bitters were built to stay out on the water for up to a week at a time, making it hard for the bootleggers and smugglers to anticipate where they might suddenly turn up. Ship to shore radio, a new technology, was installed in these ships so that they could communicate with Coast Guard stations who had information as to the possible location of rum ships. Two hundred and three of these patrol boats were built at a cost of about $35,000 each.

The other class of patrol boat, known as "picket boats," were at least as effective as the six-bitters. There were two designs. The thir-ty-five-foot version had a single cabin and open cockpit whereas the thirty-six-foot version had a double cabin with the cockpit enclosed. Both types were equipped with small arms and mounted a .30-cali-bre machine gun on the foredeck. They could make a top speed of about 24 knots (45 km/h), enabling them to outrun most rum ships on the Great Lakes. Their speed, combined with the machine gun, made them particularly effective on the Great Lakes. One hundred and three of these vessels were built at a cost of $6,800 each.

On a crisp October afternoon in 1924, the first of these new pick-et boats glided into the Coast Guard station at Oswego, New York. Captain Jackson, in charge of the Oswego station, wrote to his superintendent of this event and the lack of secrecy with some frus-tration: "Picket boat 2207 was received at this station 6 October 1924, and on that date a telegram was sent to Belleville, Ontario, the principal shipping point of liquor in eastern Lake Ontario, to the effect that boat had arrived at this station. I do not know who sent the message."[5] He went on to lament that farmers owning shoreline made more money selling landing rights to smugglers than they did from farming. He further complained that, even when caught, bootleggers were treated lightly by the courts, citing the example of one rumrunner who was fined one dollar, and when he didn't have enough money for car fare home, a collection was taken up in court which covered the cost.

Despite the frustrations of his job, Captain Jackson was encouraged by the deterrent effect the new patrol boat was having on the smugglers. The rumrunners had been avoiding the Oswego area. Only two loads had been landed in the three months since CG-2207's arrival and both had been lost to hijackers. The smugglers were naturally concerned. They did not know the capabilities of the new picket boats nor how well trained their crews would be.

Two more picket boats arrived on the Great Lakes within the month. One of these went to the Buffalo station and the other to Niagara. By 10 December 1924, there were five picket boats on the Great Lakes, all armed with .30-calibre machine guns and crewed by men anxious to engage the smugglers. For these men, the real test would not come until the following spring. On 15 December 1924, all five of the new picket boats were put into dry dock for the winter.

December fifteenth is traditionally the end of the navigation season on the Great Lakes. The lighthouses shut down, their lights are turned off, and the keepers return to the mainland and their families. Weather conditions are considered dangerous after mid-October, and insurance rates increase dramatically after mid-November. In recent years, the advent of the huge superships has changed this somewhat, but for smaller ships the situation still applies. Traditionally, the Coast Guard also takes its boats off the water when the lighthouses shut down. The severity of the weather and the lack of navigation signals creates unusually hazardous conditions for any mariners still on the lake. In the 1920s, there was no radar, no loran (a radio navigation system), almost none of the sophisticated navigation equipment which sailors today take for granted. Anyone who travelled the lake in winter was considered either foolhardy or unusually courageous. Ben Kerr was one of the few willing to challenge the winter storms and continued to cross Lake Ontario after mid December.

Kerr put the two smaller boats into dry dock at his boat house in Hamilton, but the *Martimas* was big enough and solid enough to withstand the winter storms. Moreover, Kerr had sheathed the hull in steel to prevent shore-ice from slicing through it. He did reduce the frequency of his trips, crossing the lake only two or three times a week. Moreover, he always planned his trips so that he would be in Hamilton for the Pals weekly hockey game.

Their first game of the season was on 8 January 1925 against the Bank of Montreal team. Mayor Jutten was there to drop the face-off puck. Several members of council were present as it was the start of the Industrial League's season. As usual, Ben's cheers could be heard above the din as his team went on to win three to one.[6] The Pals seemed set for a winning season.

With his expanded marine garage facilities, his three powerful boats, his winning hockey team, and his growing financial success, Kerr was, as the gamblers say, on a roll. But Lady Luck is a fickle mistress. Lulled by his successes, he seriously underestimated the United States Coast Guard. It was a mistake for which he would pay a heavy price.

Ten

John Brown Goes to Jail

The auspicious beginning of the hockey season did not hold for the Pals hockey team. They finished the season in second place, behind the Tareyton Tobacco Team who clinched the city league championship. During the season bad feelings developed between Kelly Thompson, the team's manager, and Kerr. Kelly did not drink and did not approve of Ben's practice of having the players back to his house for drinks after the game. Ben never overindulged but some of the players did. During one game the team trainer started out onto the rink and fell face down on the ice. He had enjoyed Ben's free booze to the point that the players had to help him to his feet and escort him off the rink. A religious man, Kelly disliked what was happening to the team and told Ben this. Ben told him if he didn't like it to quit, which Kelly did. Ben had to take over the manager's position. The quiet, self-effacing Kelly was replaced by the strong-willed, hard-driving Kerr.

Although the hockey season had not turned out as well for Ben as he had expected, his "liquor export" business was thriving. By 1925, he had developed a network of buyers in northern New York State. John "Butch" Schenk was the largest of these. Schenk had set up a number of bootleg centres along the shores of Lake Ontario. One of these was at the Oklahoma settlement, about seven kilometres east of the Charlotte Coast Guard station, just outside Rochester. This operation was supervised by Mae Goldstein, alias Mae Davis, alias Happy Goldstein, a tall, dark, woman in her early twenties. Mae took a taxi out to the settlement daily, overseeing the sale of the bootleg hootch, collecting the money, and returning to Rochester each night in a taxi with the money in a satchel and a large .45-calibre pistol in her lap, "just in case." Other members of the gang were Valentine Evershed, Leo Kuchert, Chris Cottrell, Clarence Heiden, and Bob Murray.

Cancelled cheques seized by American authorities reveal that Kerr and Schenk supplied numerous bootleggers in both Niagara Falls and Rochester, New York. They may also have supplied Ontario bootleggers in Niagara Falls and Toronto. Kerr had an

account with the Bank of Toronto in Trenton which he used solely
for his business with Schenk. As Kerr was buying Corby's liquor for
this part of his smuggling operation, he was by-passing Perri and
Gooderham and Worts.

Like the smuggling arrangement with Gooderham and Worts,
this system was designed to get around the niceties of the law.
Corby's distilleries did not want cheques drawn on Canadian banks
since it would appear they were selling illegally to Canadians. The
procedure was for Schenk to deposit the money to his account with
the Rochester Safe Deposit Company. Kerr would then make a draft
through the Bank of Toronto in Trenton, drawn on Schenk's bank in
Rochester. He would endorse this draft over to the brewery he was
buying from. In this way, U.S. authorities could not prove that
Schenk was buying Canadian booze as the cheques were payable to
Kerr and not a Canadian distillery or brewery.

In the spring of 1925, Ben Kerr and Alf Wheat were at the peak
of their success. Kerr had three boats crossing Lake Ontario regularly. He captained his pride, the *Martimas*, and relied on John Elliott
and John Clark as crew. He also hired some crew members in Trenton for the *Evelyn*, a beautiful open speedboat, trimmed in
mahogany. Alf Wheat captained the *Sparkley*, a thirty-six-foot twin-
engine launch, a valuable boat but not in the same class as the *Martimas*. To help Alf crew the *Sparkley*, Ben Kerr hired a Joe Thompson
from Hamilton. There is some evidence to indicate that he obtained
this last man through his friend Bill Dillon, owner of the Bayview
Hotel in Hamilton. The hotel was a popular watering hole for the
steel workers coming off shift from the rolling mills at the foot of
Queen Street. One of these was a Joe Thompson, about whom little
is known except that he worked at the steel mill for a time and then
disappeared from Hamilton.

During this period, Ben was seeing his Trenton girlfriend Kate,
and with his rumrunning crews, speeding around Trenton harbour in
his launches. He had always been something of an amateur photogra-
pher, and took pictures of the boats and his crew in Trenton harbour.
As Don Harrison remembers, "They were all having a great time. Ben
treated us to meals in the Chinese restaurant and always had a plentiful supply of liquor on board the *Martimas*. After a particularly good
week, he would sometimes break out the champagne."[1]

The Coast Guard and Custom Border Patrol were aware of his
activities but were unable to catch him. Ben held them in low regard
and openly boasted that, "I can outwit the feds anytime."[2]

Kerr and his associate, Butch Schenk, had more to contend with than U.S. law officers. There were other interests vying for control of the booze business in Rochester. Located on Cataract Street in Rochester, and owned and managed by William Rund, the Standard Brewery was ostensibly producing low alcohol beer of less than 0.5 percent alcohol for the domestic market. In fact it was producing regular beer (9 percent alcohol) with the connivance of local police and Prohibition agents.

A committee of prominent churchmen and leading citizens was so concerned with the lax enforcement of the Volstead Act in Rochester that they set up a special – albeit unofficial – organization to check up on the police and make their findings public. Calling themselves "the Committee of 25," it was headed up by several prominent citizens, including the Reverend Doctor A. W. Beaven, and attorneys William MacFarland and William Lynn. On 30 May 1925, they released a report which claimed that the brewery was being run by "certain prominent officials and politicians."[3] On the Sunday following the release of the report, the Reverend Beaven, in his Sunday sermon, flayed the city's officials for their apathy in investigating the Standard Brewery. Two years ago, he claimed when he was chairman of the Committee of 25, he had received a letter from a local bootlegger, "asking that the committee close up the Standard Brewery on the basis that only those who were willing to buy their beer from the Standard Brewery could sell without molestation in the city; that all the little bootleggers without political pull ... were being crowded out so that now the little bootlegger could no longer make an honest living."[4]

In their report the committee stated that the police and Prohibition agents knew what was going on and who was selling liquor, but for the past two years had done absolutely nothing to stop it. They claimed that, "it would be possible to close up every blind pig in Rochester within a week if the police merely gave the order to do so."[5] Closing up every speakeasy in Rochester would have been an ambitious task as the reporter Curt Gerling makes clear in his articles written some sixty years after the "Great Experiment" had ended.

Gerling lived through those days and in his retirement years wrote about them in the *Brockport Post*. He noted that all the fraternal organizations in the city had a bar and usually some slot machines. All you had to do was know someone who was a member of the Elks, or the Moose, or any of a number of fraternal organizations, and you were assured of a "wet" and lively evening. There was no shortage of "clubs." Indeed, new ones were springing up all the time.

In addition to the popular clubs, there were less reputable establishments. Known as speakeasies or blind pigs (the latter may have referred to the effect their cheap alcohol could have on a customer's eyesight). One of the more popular of these was Jim O'Brien's restaurant on Exchange Street, about half a block from the police station. It was a hang out for newspaper folk and politicians who enjoyed the relatively cheap prices and edible food. As Gerling described it:

> Jim's bunions frequently bothered him, and when the bartender showed up, the customers were served - otherwise they were often obliged to serve themselves. There were no cheques for meals. You recited what you consumed, and Jim gave you an estimate. Drinks he was less casual about.[6]

Not all speakeasies were managed with such indifference to their customers. Ward Vaughan could have competed with the best in any era. Wardie, as he was known to the multitudes who claimed his friendship, owned the Sea Glades, a Beach Avenue resort conveniently located on the shores of Lake Ontario. The Sea Glades boasted that its product was "right off the boat"; no cheap bathtub booze or watered-down drinks for their customers. Naturally, the prices reflected the high quality of the product.

An added attraction, for those with the stamina and finances to stay late enough, was the opportunity to watch an actual rumboat come in and land an illegal cargo. A natural showman, Vaughan arranged for his customers to view the landing from the Sea Glades' darkened front porch. The cruiser would come to within a hundred feet of shore, its motors muffled, its lights off, hushed voices could be heard, brief flashlight signals were glimpsed, the four rowboats manned by Wardie's employees would head out to the sandbar where the dark cruiser lay with its motors idling. They would return laden with bags of authentic Canadian whisky and ale which would be speedily taken down into the locked basement of the Sea Glades. The lights would go on and the enthralled customers could imbibe with renewed confidence that they were indeed drinking the "real stuff."

Later, the rumrunners got wind of what Wardie was doing and refused to land nearby. Not to be denied his spectacle, Wardie then "created" his own show. Using a friend's borrowed cruiser and empty whisky cases, he staged landings so convincing that few of his customers ever doubted that they were witnessing the real thing.[7] Like most of the illegal drinking establishments in Rochester, his Sea Glades survived Prohibition with little or no interference from the law. It was not the police, but the Great Depression that eventually put the genial Vaughan out of business.

Rochester was clearly a thriving market for the bootlegger. By delivering Canadian beer in large quantities to Schenk, Kerr was cutting into that market and making dangerous and powerful enemies. There is no way of proving who it was, but subsequent events suggest that the Standard Brewery interests managed to get someone inside the Schenk organization to find out when Kerr would be delivering a load of beer. They then notified the Coast Guard and Customs Border Patrol of the impending delivery. An unidentified source also notified the American consul stationed in Kingston. On 22 May 1925, Felix Johnson, American consul at Kingston, Ontario, wrote to the American secretary of state asserting that his office had secured evidence

> that may be of the greatest assistance to the American prohibition Officers.
>
> A man by the name of J.B. Kerr, who owns a motor boat, length about thirty five feet, engine 16 cylinders, finished in mahogany, under Canadian registry, is taking ale weekly, if not more, to a point near Charlotte or Sodus Point ...
>
> As soon as the boat is loaded and ready to proceed to the United States [sic] makes a draft through the Bank of Toronto at Trenton, Ontario on J.P. Schenk through the Rochester Safe Deposit Company at Rochester, N.Y. ... (My informant tells me that) ... The beer is generally brought in by automobile or trucks to Trenton for trans-shipment.[8]

The Charlotte Coast Guard station is located at the mouth of the Genesee River, near the present-day Rochester Yacht Club. One of its officers was Capt. Mason B. McCune, who, along with his two brothers, had left his father's farm near Ellisburg, New York, for a career with the Coast Guard. The youngest brother, Merle, was stationed at Oswego, and the older brother, Maurice, was stationed at Erie, Pennsylvania. All three would prove to be highly capable officers with reputations for absolute integrity. Not only could they not be bribed, they were excellent shots and good sailors.

On 29 April 1925, picket boat 2330, arrived at the Charlotte Coast Guard station. It was a thirty-six footer, equipped with two enclosed cabins, and requiring a crew of only three men. Capt. Mason McCune was placed in charge of its first few shake down cruises.

Ben Kerr and the rumrunning fraternity were aware of the danger posed by these new boats, although it is unlikely they knew their exact capabilities. The Martimas had a maximum speed of from 15 to 18 knots (28–33 km/h), about the same speed as the patrol boats (six-bitters), but would not be able to outrun the much faster picket boats. Kerr resolved to rely on his skill and guile to elude the Coast Guard's picket boats. He had reason to believe that would be enough. Many of them poorly trained and inexperienced sailors. All during the fall of 1924 and the spring of 1925, Kerr and his men had eluded the picket boat stationed at Oswego. In the words of the Custom Border Patrol, "he always landed where we least expected."[9]

Although slower than Kerr's two speedboats, the Martimas had the advantage of a much greater carrying capacity. A hundred cases was the average load for a speedboat, but the Martimas could carry as many as 1,200 cases of beer. At that time, beer came in quarts and a case consisted of a dozen twenty-two ounce bottles, packed in a card board box. Whisky came packed in a wooden case. Neither container was suitable for rumrunning. They were hard to pack efficiently in the rounded hull of a boat, and the whisky cases had the added disadvantage of floating when thrown overboard. A pursuing Coast Guard vessel needed to pick up only one case for the court to have the necessary proof.

Most rumrunners packed their cargo in burlap bags. They were easy to pack and handle – and didn't float. One of the many tricks used by the rumrunners was to tie a cord to the bags of booze so that they were all connected. If they had to throw a cargo overboard, they could drag for it latter, knowing that when they found one bag, they had found them all. Another ploy was to tie a marker to an empty bag and weigh it down with a block of salt. When the salt melted, the bag would pop to the surface; its marker made the bags of beer easy to find.

Kerr had certain rules he followed to avoid detection and capture. He frequently changed his drop days and absolutely refused to land on the American shore. This gave him a better opportunity to make a run for it if detected. A boat which had landed took longer to get out and moving. He also refused to travel under a full moon, preferring dark, foggy, or hazy nights.

Once in American waters, he doused his running lights. All his boats were painted black to make detection at night even more difficult. Until late May of 1925, these methods had been effective. But, they could not protect him from moles.

In the late afternoon of 26 May, the *Martimas* left Port Hope harbour carrying 1,200 cases of Canadian ale destined for the Oklahoma settlement near Rochester. Kerr had loaded the beer at Trenton, but as Canada Customs was required to notify the Americans of all boats leaving port with booze, Ben had put in at Port Hope for a few days hoping to throw the Americans off the scent. John Elliott and John Clark were on board to assist in unloading and to help Kerr in protecting the cargo. For protection, the *Martimas* carried a .45-calibre automatic revolver, a 12-gauge shotgun and a repeating Winchester rifle.

In Rochester, certain law enforcement agencies had been tipped off and were ready. Andrew Wiedenmann, chief collector of customs for the port of Rochester, commanded a joint land and sea operation, involving the Coast Guard, Customs Border Patrol, and Prohibition agents. Wiedenmann gave the Coast Guard extra support by placing Customs Officer Mockridge onboard Coast Guard picket boat 2330 which was under the command of Mason McCune, and manned by mechanic Lindsey and surfman Wilzin. It is possible that Wiedenmann didn't trust the Coast Guard and put Mockridge on board to ensure full cooperation. The Rochester and state police were not involved in the operation, indicating Wiedenmann was aware of the corruption rampant in both forces.

On shore, Wiedenmann commanded a force of automobiles, trucks, and about twenty men. The automobiles were to patrol the roads surrounding the Oklahoma settlement which was where Wiedenmann had been told the drop was to be made. A system of signals had been worked out with the Coast Guard crew so that the officers on shore could signal the picket boat crew to close in when the moment was right.

In the early hours of the morning, the customs officers spotted the *Martimas* moored outside a small inlet offshore from the Oklahoma settlement. A dory was being used to transfer bags of ale from the *Martimas* to shore, where the bags were unloaded and pulled back to the *Martimas* by Kerr and his crew to be reloaded. Wiedenmann signalled to Mason McCune on picket boat 2330. McCune was about a mile from the little inlet when he received the signal. He immediately headed for the drop point at full speed. Sensing danger, Kerr cut his lines and, with three men from the loading party still on board, headed back for the Canadian side with engines at full throttle. All the lights on the *Martimas* had been doused to avoid detection. Had Kerr been alerted a minute or two earlier, McCune would have been unable to spot the *Martimas*, which would have been far enough out on the lake to be invisible to the naked eye. But McCune spotted the black ship and gave chase, gradually overtaking the bigger and slower *Martimas*. As soon as Kerr realized he had been spotted, he gave the order to jettison the cargo. Five men were desperately throwing bags of beer overboard as the picket boat drew close.

As they drew alongside, McCune hailed the rum ship to "heave to" but Kerr ignored him, continuing at full speed for the Canadian side, hoping to give his men enough time to get the cargo overboard. McCune ordered several shots fired over the bows of the *Martimas*. When that failed, he ordered a round from the machine gun to be fired into the boat's hull. At that, Kerr slowed the *Martimas* somewhat, still hoping to delay long enough for his men to get the last of the beer overboard. But the large, slow moving, *Martimas* gave McCune the opportunity he needed. Two of his more athletic crew members leaped to the deck of the black ship where they found the rumrunners busily throwing the last few bags overboard. The coast guardsmen fired their pistols over the heads of the smugglers, ordering them to freeze. There were just eight bags left, but that was more than enough to prove that the men had been smuggling. Kerr had not been able to delay quite long enough.

While this was going on, Wiedenmann and his officers had sped down the dirt road toward the inlet where the *Martimas* had been unloading. They drove under the railroad bridge and turned into the Oklahoma settlement where they found their path blocked by what they thought was a man in overalls, wearing a slouch hat pulled down over his face. Inspector Devaney got out of the car and approached this person, ordering him to throw up his hands. At close range, the mysterious bootlegger made a sudden grab for a revolver tucked inside the overalls. Devaney grabbed the gun – a fully loaded .45 automatic revolver – and discovered that he had arrested a young woman. She was Mae Goldstein, alias Mae Davis, alias "Happy" Goldstein, and she refused to answer any questions.

Two members of the bootlegging gang, Chris Cottrell and Valentine Evershed, were captured trying to escape. They had been down at the shore helping to unload the dory as it came in with each load of beer. Butch Schenk and Bob Murray (an alias), were holed up in a cottage which was being used as their distribution centre. Wiedenmann placed a cordon of thirteen armed men around the cottage while he went for a search warrant. This was in the early morning hours of Wednesday, 27 May, but it was not until mid-morning that the search warrant was obtained. The customs officers had to wait outside the cottage for about ten hours before Wiedenmann showed up with the search warrant. Once that had been obtained, the men inside, Schenk and Murray, quickly surrendered and were taken to the Monroe County lock up.

Inside the cottage, the customs officers found six hundred cases of beer, two automatic shotguns, two rifles, one automatic pistol, and a double-barrelled shotgun. Three of the weapons were fully loaded. In a shed near the cottage, the officers found a large jug of gin, a jug of wine, and eight cases of Corby's whisky. On the dory which Kerr had cut loose when he made his dash to escape, the Coast Guard found another sixty bags of ale. The cottage also contained an ice-box full of beer, and a cash register containing a considerable sum of money. These items supported the information supplied to Wiedenmann that the cottage was being used as a kind of retail liquor store. Three trucks were used to haul the confiscated beer, liquor, and weapons into Rochester for storage at the Customs offices. Expecting to find a cache of drugs, the officers then tore up the floor boards of the cottage as well as the inside walls but only found more liquor.

The *Rochester Democrat and Times* hailed the capture, proclaiming in a large headline that, "KING OF LAKE RUM RING CAPTURED." A great deal of interest was shown in Kerr, alias John Brown, who was constantly referred to as the, "KING RUM RUNNER." Customs officials were quoted in the Rochester Democrat and Chronicle, stating that:

Kerr is the most daring rumrunner on the lake. For the past three years the Federal men have been laying for him at various points along the lake but always he would appear where they least expected him. Last summer he piloted a mysterious black boat, unloading large cargoes at various points along the lake shore between Rochester and Pultneyville.

On Thursday 28 May, bail was set for the seven Americans captured at $5,000 each. Ben Kerr and his two Canadian crewmen had their bail set at $10,000 each (worth about $200,000 today). Neither John Clark nor John Elliott had that kind of money, and Kerr was unwilling to pay it. Nor was Mae Davis initially able to make bail. There was a great deal of interest in Davis, who was described as tall with short-bobbed dark hair. The press noted that she was the first woman rumrunner to be captured in the Rochester area. It was only six years since women had been able to vote in an Ontario election, and they were still regarded as the weaker sex. The notion that a woman might go about armed with a large revolver, engaging in the dangerous business of rumrunning was strange in the extreme. On 29 May, the *Democrat and Chronicle* commented that:

> Meanwhile the mysterious Mae Davis, captured with the rumrunners, repels all attempts to make her talk as she passes the time in the County jail. And the legends of her prowess go on. Each story eclipses the last, until it seems quite certain that the rum-running "virago" will become the most picturesque figure in the Lake Ontario rum fleet before the trial. Each hour brings a fresh story of her courage in facing the approaching customs men and her fearlessness as she reigned among the visitors to the ale cache of the "gang."
>
> According to visitors to the cottage at Oklahoma, "Happy" ... was by turns the head of the house, the chief salesman, the "officer" in charge of unloading incoming cargoes, and the hostess at the "wild parties" that are said to have followed each successful landing.[10]

Kerr and Schenk may have been amused by all the attention paid to Mae Davis by the press. They may also have suspected that "Happy" was the mole inside their organization. Her reaching for her weapon when she was already looking into the gun of Inspector Devaney was either extremely foolhardy or a signal to Devaney that this was the right place. Of the ten people arrested, she was the only one against whom charges were dropped. As overseer of the Oklahoma operation, she had advance information available to very few members of the gang. In particular, she would have known some time in advance when the delivery was to take place. After the trial, she conveniently disappeared.[11]

Schenk's mother came forward and, using her home and two lots as security, was able to make bond for her son. Considering that the twenty-six-year-old Schenk was clearly the organizer of a large bootlegging ring, her comments to the press reaffirm the old adage that there is nothing so blind as a mother's love.

Questioned by a reporter as they left the County jail, Schenk's mother told the newshound that: "I don't want anyone to call Elmer a rumrunner. He has been driving a truck for several years and has always been a good boy. He was offered $15 for a few minutes work and was weak enough to accept it. I'm sure Elmer didn't intend to do any great wrong." The reporter noted that Elmer's mother wanted her son to come home, but Elmer insisted on staying in Rochester.

The evening prior to Elmer "Butch" Schenk's release, two people had been seen running away from the Standard Brewery on Cataract Street. A few minutes later, two dynamite explosions did considerable damage to the structure. The rumrunners were blaming the brewery's owners for tipping off the Coast Guard and Customs officials. Clearly the bootlegging war was heating up. Unfortunately for Kerr and his fellow inmates at the County jail, the weather was just as hot.

Two days after the rumrunners' capture, Rochester found itself in the grip of the worst heatwave on record to that time. Air conditioning had not yet been invented. The only way to escape the debilitating heat was to be on or in the water. Rochestarians by the thousands flocked to Lake Ontario's beaches to cool off. Many of these were the same beaches the rumrunners had been using for their deliveries. Ben Kerr was put to work in the blazing heat, weeding onions on the prison farm. He was waiting for his lawyer to negotiate a lower bail. It is unlikely that Kerr could not arrange the bail. It is more likely that he was already considering the possibility of forfeiting bail rather than serve time in an American prison.

Day after day, the incredible heat went on; schools were closed as were many factories, offices and stores. At Columbus, Ohio, the thermometer reached 105°F (40°C). Elderly people and those without the means to leave the city began collapsing and some died. Over a twenty-four hour period on Sunday, 7 June, seventy people in the U.S. died from the heat. On the same day seven people died from heat prostration in Rochester.

On 9 June rain came, bringing relief to the entire north-eastern United States. Kerr's lawyer finally managed to reduce his bail from

$10,000 to $5,000, and he was released on 16 June. Neither the heat nor the jail appears to have diminished his spirit. Prohibition agents accompanied him to Buffalo where he announced to the fascinated press that he was returning to the "ale fleet," he then turned and strode into Canada.[12]

It was sheer bravado for Kerr to make such a statement and indicates that he had already decided to forfeit his bail money. He had suffered a major setback with the capture of the *Martimas* and the loss of its cargo. The Coast Guard conservatively estimated the *Martimas* to be worth a minimum of $11,000, and the retail value of the cargo at $17,000. Then there was the $5,000 in bail money which his lawyer had paid to the court, consisting of $4,500 in Victory Bonds and a certified cheque for $500. In today's depreciated currency, the loss would amount to about $650,000.

The publicity accorded his capture now made Kerr a major target of the United States Coast Guard who were proving to be a dangerous foe. Ben had made opponents of the McCune brothers who were every bit as capable and as determined as himself. No longer would he scoff at the feds. They now had the equipment to drive all but the most capable and well equipped rumrunners off the lakes. This fact became increasingly apparent over the next few years as a dangerous shooting war developed between the remaining smugglers and the determined members of the Coast Guard. Kerr and Wheat continued on, increasingly aware that the odds were turning against them.

Eleven

Five Thousand Dollars
for Charity

Just before nightfall on Saturday, 6 June, less than two weeks before Ben Kerr got out on bail, a sleek, powerful, seventy-five-foot patrol boat arrived at the Charlotte Coast Guard station, just outside Rochester. It was the second of the new patrol boats to be posted to the Great Lakes. Chief Boatswain Kalinski and a crew of seven manned *CG-131* which was equipped with two one thousand-gallon gasoline tanks, enabling it to roam over Lake Ontario for up to a week at a time without putting into port. The ship came equipped with sleeping quarters for the men, a powerful search light, and radio equipment that allowed it to keep abreast of intelligence information as to the activities of rumrunners. Weighing in at seventy-five tons, it was equipped with a 37-mm gun (or one-pound cannon) which was accurate over a range of two miles (3.2 km). Mounted on the foredeck with the cannon was a .30-calibre Lewis machine gun, the same kind that had been used by aircraft during the Great War with such dead-ly effect. Capable of a top speed of from 15 to 18 knots (28 to 33 km/h), it was fast enough to catch most of the rum ships on the lake.[1]

What was most disturbing to the bootlegging fraternity was their inability to know where *CG-131* might be at any given time. This ele-ment of surprise resulted in several captures of rum ships on the Great Lakes during 1925.

In the early years of Prohibition, a favourite tactic of the large-scale liquor interests (including the Bronfmans and Corby's) was to send large quantities of their product to Halifax by train where it would be transferred to oceangoing sailing vessels. The rum ships would then take their cargoes to the Atlantic waters off the coasts of New York, Boston, Long Island, and New Jersey. The ships' captains were careful to stay far enough off shore to be in international waters and therefore exempt from seizure by the U.S. Navy or Coast Guard. These ships waited outside the international limit for their customers (usually organized gangsters) to send out fast launches to load up with a hundred or so cases which they would then bring back to the eastern seaboard, relying on their superior speed and the cover of darkness to elude the Coast Guard.

Until 1924, the United States Coast Guard was virtually power-less to stop this traffic. In that year, President Coolidge sent supple-mental estimates to Congress of $13.9 million for the purpose of strengthening the Coast Guard. A portion of this money was to be spent on reconditioning twenty World War I destroyers and two mine sweepers, which the President had transferred to the Coast Guard from the U.S. Navy, as well as constructing patrol and picket boats for use on the Great Lakes. The president also recommended to Congress that additional officers and men be recruited into the Coast Guard on a temporary basis. On 2 April 1924, the United States Congress approved the president's requests. Work began almost immediately on the new patrol boats and in reconditioning the destroyers, many of which had deteriorated badly since the war. Late in the summer of that year, the first of these destroyers was put to sea.

The Coast Guard was helped enormously in its struggle against the "rummies" by a treaty reached between the United States and Great Britain in May of 1924. Previous to this treaty, the four-mile limit was the distance from shore a boat had to maintain to remain in international waters. As long as the big liquor supply ships kept out-side that distance they could not be seized. But the treaty recognized a new limit of one hour's steaming time from shore. In practice, this forced the mother ships to moor from thirty to forty miles out from shore as many of their contact boats could travel fast enough to cover that distance in an hour.

The tactics of the reorganized force was to shadow or "picket" any rum ships found off the U.S. coast. Any contact boat loaded with contraband knew that the destroyer would be using its radio to give a description and probable destination of the contact boat to the inshore patrol boats. The increased distance from shore gave the speedy patrol boats a better chance to intercept the rum boats before they could land.

The annual report of the Coast Guard for the year 1925 gives an overall view of the progress achieved in the first year. Recruiting cen-tres had been opened in Baltimore, Boston, New York, Norfolk, and Philadelphia. In the first forty-five days of the recruiting drive, the force had been expanded from 3,745 to over 5,000 enlisted men. The navy was assisting in the training of these new recruits, many of whom had never been to sea. By the end of 1925, the twenty destroy-ers were fully operational and all 203 of the new patrol boats had been completed and were in service. Captures of rum ships increased dramatically.

There were some problems. The report noted that only a few vessels had been able to hold small arms practice, that no vessels had been able to hold great (large) gun practice, that the radio equipment on practically all the destroyers was fast becoming obsolete, and that it needed extra funds to replace the 3- and 4-inch ammunition which had been furnished by the Navy free of charge, but was now depleted. Despite these problems the report was able to state that "the notorious rum row, formerly lying off the entrance to New York, and off Long Island and New Jersey, has been effectively scattered."[2]

This achievement enabled the Coast Guard to divert more of its resources to the Great Lakes. Patrol Boat *131* was diverted from the Atlantic coast to the Charlotte station on Lake Ontario. Its sister ship, *CG-121*, was posted to the Erie station in May and quickly demonstrated the effectiveness of the new six-bitters. On May the sixteenth, *CG-121* captured a motorboat, its crew, and 350 cases of Canadian ale. Three weeks later, the patrol boat fired several rounds at a speedy rum ship, forcing its crew to surrender. On board the rum boat, the coast guardsmen found 700 cases of Canadian ale. In July, the patrol boat captured two more rum ships and several hundred cases of Canadian ale. In September the crew of *CG-121* seized yet another "black," which was the Coast Guard's code name for a rumrunner.[3]

Ben Kerr and the other rumrunners were keenly aware that the days of easy money were over. Only the more capable seamen were willing to carry on smuggling under the new conditions. Don Harrison of Trenton was one of those who decided it was too dangerous an occupation. He quit after the summer of 1925. "It wasn't just the Coast Guard," he recalled, "some of the guys you had to deal with on the other [U.S.] side were awful tough." Harrison frequently worked for Wild Bill Sheldon "who," he stated, "would cross the lake in weather that wasn't fit for man nor beast ... I figured that if I didn't drown ... one day, one of those guys [American gangsters] was going to blast me to kingdom come. So I got out." Harrison remembers that Wild Bill was "too crazy to quit" and "Kerr ... well that man, he wasn't afraid of nobody, no sir, not him."[4]

Contrary to Don Harrison's opinion, Kerr was quite concerned over the prospect of going back to jail. Rather than return directly to smuggling, the evidence suggests he began hiring others to do the job. In the early morning hours of 24 June 1925, a week after Kerr had posted bail and had been released, Alf Wheat and Joe Thompson

headed across Lake Ontario in the *Sparkley*, carrying a heavy load of
800 cases of Cosgraves ale. They were to land at Nine Mile Point,
about seven miles from Rochester, not far from the Oklahoma settlement. Once again the Customs officers appear to have been tipped
off. Both they and Mason McCune, in picket boat *2330*, were lying in
wait. When most of the cargo had been transferred to the two trucks,
the Cadillac sedan, and the Studebaker touring car, the agents
swooped in on the gang on the beach. They had already signalled
McCune who moved in to block off any escape by the *Sparkley*.

Alf and another of the bootleg party fled into the woods amidst
a hail of bullets from the customs men. The rest, including Joe
Thompson, were captured.[5] The cargo was valued at more than ten
thousand dollars while the Coast Guard put a value of twenty-five
hundred dollars on the thirty-six-foot, twin-engine motor launch. It
was another expensive set back for Kerr.[6]

There is no evidence as to the identity of the informant tipping off
the Customs Service. The two most likely sources were the Standard
Brewery interests and Rocco Perri. Just two months earlier, Rocco and
Bessie had pressured Gooderham and Worts to stop supplying Kerr.
They had been successful, but Kerr had continued buying from
Corby's distillery in Belleville. At the time of the *Martimas* capture, cus-
toms agents had found eight cases of whisky – all of it from Corby's.

Kerr's setbacks continued. John Clark and John Elliott, the two
men captured with him on the *Martimas*, had earlier pleaded guilty
and received two months each. While in the county lock-up, they had
become chatty with one of the guards, telling him about an incident
which occurred in the summer of the previous year. They had been
travelling late at night in the *Martimas* and were near Main Duck
Island when they heard a crash at the stern of their vessel. They
turned on their search light in time to see two men in a small craft
which, in the inky blackness, had crashed into their stern. Before any
action could be taken, the boat and its occupants had vanished under
the waves. It was a stormy night, but as they were still in American
waters, Kerr had kept his running lights off – a clear violation of the
law of the sea. The two victims, Harry Sheldon and David Tugwell,
were well known residents of Oswego, New York. American officials
told the press that they were considering charging Ben Kerr with
manslaughter.[7] If Kerr had been considering appearing for trial, this
certainly changed his mind.

The trial of the smugglers was held at Canandaigua, New York,
on 23 September 1925. Unlike some of his associates, Judge John R.

Hazel was known to be tough on large-scale smugglers. John "Butch" Schenk received a year and a day in a prison at Atlanta. U.S. Attorney Richard Templeton described the other defendants as merely workers for Kerr. They each received sixty days in the county lock-up. Charges against Mae Davis were dismissed for lack of evidence; a strange thing, given the eyewitness accounts of her presence at the site, and Inspector Devaney's grabbing of the .45-calibre automatic out of her hand. She had been charged with carrying a concealed weapon and was clearly guilty.

As Kerr did not appear for sentencing, the United States marshall in Rochester began proceedings to escheat the bail money posted by Kerr. Judge Hazel also ordered that the *Martimas* be turned over to Andrew Wiedenmann, the U.S. Customs Collector for Rochester. The standard procedure had been for the Customs Office to advertise the "black ships" for sale at public auction. The former owner of the boat, or someone acting for him, would often come to the auction and buy it back for a fraction of its true value, intending to put it back into service as a rumrunner. But Wiedenmann frustrated Kerr's plans by turning the *Martimas* over to the Coast Guard who planned to use it to catch smugglers.

A few weeks before the trial at Canandaigua, rumrunner Charlie Mills was captured by Merle McCune (the brother of Kerr's captor) in picket boat *2207*, near Oswego. Mills, who was an American, put up $3,000 in bail money and pleaded not guilty. Later, he was found guilty, fined $10,000 and sentenced to a year in prison at Atlanta. In earlier years, smugglers had been tried under the Volstead Act. The act treated the offence as a misdemeanour, but increasingly judges were convicting them with smuggling and conspiracy under the Tariff and Customs laws, which were indictable offenses carrying stiff sentences and larger fines.

A further seizure was made by the intrepid Mason McCune that fall. Accompanied by surfmen Duzell, Matteson, and Perry, in picket boat *2330*, Captain McCune was cruising about five-and-a-half miles east of the Oklahoma settlement when he spotted a black ship which he quickly overtook and captured. The launch was carrying 125 cases of Frontenac Canadian ale. The Customs Officials on shore arrested three men and seized two cars and one truck. The crew of the black ship consisted of Earl D. Woodward of Rochester, and Fred Brooks of Brighton, Ontario.[8]

Kerr could not be tied directly to this boat but it fits the description of the boat the American Consul in Kingston had earlier described as operating from Trenton. Kerr would certainly know men in both Rochester and Brighton. The landing destination, near Oklahoma, where the *Martimas* was captured earlier, suggests that Kerr had lost yet another boat.

If it was Kerr's boat, it indicates a change in tactics. This last boat was worth considerably less than the others. Many rumrunners tried to minimize their losses by using cheaper boats and carrying smaller cargoes. If they lost one boat in ten trips, they were still ahead financially. As these boats, if detected, were too slow to elude the Coast Guard, the owners usually hired others to drive them. These men, called "pullers," were paid between twenty-five and a hundred dollars per trip. In 1925, the boat owners were being paid from two to three dollars a case. The profit on 125 cases would therefore be from $250 to $375, from which the owner would pay the two pullers a total of about one hundred dollars. The men hired to drive these boats were usually found around the docks, and while they often had experience on the lake, were usually unskilled workers for whom fifty dollars represented two week's wages. Besides, the courts regarded them as small fry and tended to treat them leniently if captured.

The usual pattern among rumrunners was to start out driving someone else's boat, and then graduate to driving their own for much bigger profits. Those, who could resist blowing their profits by living life in the "fast lane," might then graduate to hiring others to drive their boat or boats. One of these was the Belleville veterinarian, Hedley Welbanks. The industrious "Doc" started out in the early days of Prohibition, driving his own boat. As a veterinarian, he was permitted by the Ontario Temperance Act to carry up to a quart of whisky with him on his rounds; it being commonly believed that whisky could revive a sick horse. This enabled Doc Welbanks to develop a thriving rural bootlegging business. By the time the Coast Guard had become a serious threat on Lake Ontario, the veterinarian had amassed enough money to hire others to drive his various boats. He also acted as an organizer of the fishermens' rum fleet which operated out of the Quinte area for Corby's distillery. He was well known in the area for his famous "Doctor Welbanks' White Liniment," which he sold for five dollars a quart. The "Doc" could buy raw alcohol exempt from the usual government taxes for "medicinal purposes" at just $2.60 a gallon. His "liniment" was made from raw alcohol diluted with two parts water. A quart of raw alcohol cost Welbanks about twenty-five cents and the glass bottle and label slightly more.

At five dollars a quart, the good doctor was making almost as much mark-up as some of todays' pharmaceutical manufacturers.

In the early days of Prohibition, the burly veterinarian was an occasional visitor to Main Duck Island. He had been born and raised on a farm in Prince Edward County, and knew many of the fishermen who worked there. During the 1920s, the fishing industry collapsed, and Welbanks was able to recruit some of these sturdy sailors into the service of himself and Corby's distillery. As a rumrunner, Welbanks was not in a class with Kerr. He was not an experienced sailor and never risked investing in a large and powerful boat comparable to the *Martimas*. The boats used by the men hired by "Doc" Welbanks could be bought for less than five hundred dollars.

Kerr probably decided to refrain from operating any black ships himself until the outcome of his legal move to regain his bail money. Not only did this fail but the United States Department of Justice began proceedings to extradite him to stand trial for "conspiracy to violate the Tariff Act, the National Prohibition Act, with smuggling, and with transporting and possessing in violation of the Tariff Act."[9] As Kerr later told Jack Morris Jr., "if they ever catch me, they're going to throw away the key."

In December of that year, Kerr found himself in the headlines once again. He was one of a number of Canadians and Americans named in forty-three warrants for arrest issued in New York City by Gen. Lincoln C. Andrews, in charge of Prohibition enforcement, and U.S. Attorney Emory R. Buckner. One of the men arrested was the millionaire business and sportsman, William Dwyer, half owner of the Mount Royal racetrack in Montreal, and half owner of the Coney Island racetrack in Cincinnati. Described as "the King of the Canadian Liquor Runners," Kerr was accused by the United States Customs with landing large cargoes of champagne near Rochester.

Interviewed at his Bay Street office by the *Hamilton Herald*, Ben denied the charges, claiming that he had not been in American waters since the 25 May, when he had been captured. This was probably true. It was probably also true that, using others to drive his boats, he was sending champagne into the Rochester area. But Kerr was still smarting over his losses and could not resist throwing down the gauntlet. "Tell the coast guard," he said, "to put up or shut up. I'll make this offer: If any American Prohibition officer can prove that I have been in American waters since 25 May last, I will hand over $5,000 to any Hamilton charitable institution to be named by the official. As for champagne," he continued, "you can tell the world, I don't even know what champagne looks like."[10] Don Harrison, his friend in Trenton, knew otherwise.

Although still defiant of authority, Kerr had become more cautious, less willing to take the physical risks himself. To avoid capture by the Coast Guard, he had ordered a new boat from his friend Jack Morris. This boat, which he named the "Pollywog," would be faster than any of his previous boats. With its unusual design, the *Pollywog* might well have been the fastest rumrunner on the lakes. Ben Kerr would get back into rumrunning when he believed he could outrun the Coast Guard – and not before.

Twelve

Hockey and Homicide

Records seized from the Gooderham and Worts distillery confirm that even after his arrest in the summer of 1925, Kerr was still in the liquor export business. Either he or Alf Wheat was delivering an average of seventy-five cases of whisky weekly to a bootlegger in Olcott, New York. The lake smugglers usually did much more business in ale than in whisky, and while no records of Ben's ale business exists, it is almost certain that he was also delivering Canadian ale to American bootleggers. The distillery's records show Kerr picking up eighty cases of whisky at a cost of $2,325, paid for by an M. Wilkes of Olcott, on 22 December 1925. This was his last delivery for the year, and indeed, for several months.

Lacking a boat equipped to operate on the lake in winter, Ben turned his energy to the Pals hockey team. He had sponsored it for several years and had been a regular and enthusiastic supporter at every game. In the winter of 1925–26, he became its manager. Not surprisingly, it turned out to be a memorable season.

The season's first game was played on 7 December 1925 with the Pals defeating the previous year's champs, the Tucketts, by a convincing score of 7 to 1. Ben was there, cheering on his team, and thoroughly enjoying the challenge. "We are going to win it all," he is reported to have exhorted his players during their rout of the former city champions.[1]

The team began to reflect Ben's intensely competitive nature. He was a hard driver. If a player did not maintain his best level of play during a game, Ben took him aside for a talk. A perfectionist, he demanded the same from his players. They were amateurs, receiving not a dime for their efforts, but Ben fired them up with his enthusiasm and confidence. By 27 February 1926, the team had amassed thirty-one points, their closest rival the Tucketts had only nineteen. The Pals, also called the "sailors," had already wrapped up the league title with two more games to be played.[2]

Hamilton sports fans had been frustrated by the loss of their Intermediate OHA team a few years earlier, and by the loss of their NHL team at the end of the previous season. They transferred their interest to the Pals and the teams in the city and commercial leagues. In the previous season the teams in these leagues had their scores published but otherwise received little coverage. In the 1925–26 season, this changed dramatically, with "Ben Kerr's sailors" getting a lot of ink on the pages of the *Hamilton Spectator*. The regular league schedule called for one game a week for each team, but Ben worked his players extra hard by arranging exhibition games with teams from other leagues, usually from the Intermediate Ontario Hockey League. This league was considered much superior in skills to the level of hockey found in city and commercial leagues, but the Pals' team invariably won these contests, sparking further interest in the "plucky sailors."

At the close of the regular season, Kerr continued this policy, keeping his team sharp for the city championship series with Westinghouse, the Commercial League champions. He also issued a challenge to the Guelph team, winners of the Intermediate OHA, who declined on account of injuries. The Jordan team had finished second to Guelph, but they too declined. Dunnville, the third-place team, accepted Kerr's challenge, perhaps because Ben and Louisa were developing a reputation for hospitality; the visitors were invited to the Kerr home for a "hearty and delicious" dinner before the game. The Pals were also there for the dinner. After the game, which the Pals won handily, Kerr invited both teams back for drinks and a convivial evening. It is likely that Ben or Louisa played the piano during the sing songs referred to in the newspaper. He and Louisa May continued this policy at all of the Pal's exhibition games. When the Pals lost, as they did against an all-star team from Burlington, Kerr took the players aside individually and extracted a promise from each that, "they would play the best hockey they were capable of."[3] In the return match with the Burlington team, the sailors won 4 to 2.

After five exhibition games and four victories, against either out of town all-star teams or Intermediate OHA teams, the Pals finally faced off against Westinghouse, winners of the Commercial League. Westinghouse never had much of a chance, losing both games in the two game series. The Pals had won the city championship and with it Colonel Grafton's silver cup. What the Colonel thought when he handed the trophy to Kerr, notorious rumrunner, is unfortunately not recorded.

As the press had been reporting, there was considerable discussion during the season that the Pals would be applying for entry into the Intermediate OHA league. To back up this application, Ben believed they must first win the city championship and then challenge the best team in the Intermediate OHA. He was so confident of winning the city title, he issued the challenge before the series with Westinghouse had begun. Just three days after the series with Westinghouse, the Pals faced off against the Grimsby Peach Kings, considered a powerhouse, and winners of the league title for the past two years. The game was played in the old Barton Street Arena on 24 March 1925, and was the feature story on the sports pages the next day. The *Spectator* reporter noted that:

> although they met and defeated several strong outside teams, they (the Pals) had never been previously tested until last night. Against the Grimsby Peach Kings, however, the Sailors fully demonstrated their ability ... The largest crowd of the season, about 1,500, saw the sailors battle to a 5-5 tie.[4]

The reporter commented on the classy play of the Peach Kings but credited the Pals with "oodles of energy and a determination to win." Ben's contribution to the team had been to imbue them with his own qualities of determination, perseverance, and confidence.

After the game, Ben and Louisa had the players back to the house on Bay Street North for a stag at which they discussed the possibility of entering a team in the Intermediate League the next year. At the end of the evening the *Spectator* noted that "a very hearty vote of thanks was passed to Manager Kerr and to Mrs. Kerr, whose efforts to entertain the players this season could not have been surpassed."[5]

This joint effort by Ben and Louisa May reflects what was possibly one of the happiest times in their marriage. In this period, their relationship appears to have developed into a sound working and affectionate partnership. Unfortunately, no letters or written documents survive to substantiate this, but Louisa May kept all her photos and that collection survives to this day. For the first time since their wedding, there are pictures of the two of them together, and they look happy. Their daughter, Helen, is in these photos and the pose suggests an affectionate bond between father and daughter. It was about this time that Ben decided to build a house next to their home on Bay Street. Mother and daughter were unusually close. Ben told them that he was building the house so that Helen could live there when she grew up and married.

It was a golden period for both of them. Ben threw himself into the Pals team and Louisa joined in, sharing with him in the excitement of the competition. For a little while, during that winter, she no longer had to worry about Ben's survival on the lake or about his being arrested and jailed by the Americans. No doubt she wanted this lifestyle to continue, but she was a passive woman and against the dominant will of Ben stood no chance of persuading him to quit.

She could have made a strong case for him to retire from the liquor export business. Their boat storage and repair business was doing well, their two houses were paid for, one of these provided them with a monthly rent, and most importantly for Louisa, the liquor business was more dangerous than it had ever been. Increasingly, it had come to be dominated by gangsters like Perri and Al Capone, and by psychopathic killers such as Jack "Legs" Diamond, and Dutch Schultz. Louisa and Ben both came from respectable middle-class families, and the association with violent criminals was no doubt embarrassing to them both. As subsequent events would show, it was certainly embarrassing to Louisa May. There was also the argument of age. In that generation, middle age arrived by the time one turned forty. Ben turned forty-two that February. He was at least a decade older than most of the active rumrunners on the lake. But Ben was anxious to recoup some of the losses of the previous summer. Moreover, the favourable press attending the Pals' victories had blotted out much of the negative publicity he had received over his arrest in Rochester the previous May. He undoubtedly believed that his abilities as a mariner and the unusually fast boat ordered from Jack Morris would enable him to elude the U.S. Coast Guard and his other enemies.

Records seized from Gooderham and Worts Distillery reveal that Kerr began making deliveries of their product on 16 April 1926. The hockey season was over, but more importantly, the ice was out of Hamilton harbour, making it possible for his new boat, the *Pollywog*, to leave Kerr Marine and travel via the Burlington canal to Lake Ontario. Industrial discharge prevents the harbour from freezing over today, but in the 1920s, it still froze up in winter. Sometime that winter, while the harbour was still frozen, Ben took delivery of the *Pollywog* from the Morris Boat Works. The exact date of delivery is not known, but the photo of the *Pollywog* behind Kerr's home, with Jack Morris Jr. standing at the bow, is almost certainly taken at the time of delivery.

The boat has been towed on a sled from the boat works along the ice to a spot in front of Kerr Marine by the horse shown in the photograph. Young Morris has brought it down, and Kerr, who enjoyed taking photographs of his boats, has captured the moment. Note that the hull of the boat has the usual V shape at the bow, but flattens out about half way back. Fishermen called this a "tumbling stern." This design, novel in the 1920s, was the forerunner of modern racing boat design. It enables a large boat to "plane": when the bow is thrust up by the resistance of the water as the boat gains speed, the stern, which in normal designs would be thrust deeper into the water, rides up on top. This greatly reduces drag and allows the boat to reach much greater speeds than craft with conventional hulls. Kerr installed two 180 horsepower Kermath engines, weighing between 800 to 1,000 pounds each. The combination of these powerful engines with the hull design enabled the boat to reach speeds of 40 MPH (65 km/h). The *Pollywog* was forty feet in length with a beam of approximately seven feet. Although the hull was sheathed in steel to protect it from ice, the *Pollywog* was not particularly sturdy; it was built for speed.[6]

Kerr planned to captain it himself. He did not have much confidence in others driving his boats. Alf Wheat had an abundance of courage but was not a skilled mariner. Moreover, "Gunner" Wheat was fully occupied with his two trucks running beer, and his weekly trips in Ben's smaller boat to Olcott, New York. Throughout the spring and summer, Kerr piloted the *Pollywog* alone, gambling that his knowledge of the lake and the speed of the *Pollywog* would give him the edge over an increasingly dangerous Coast Guard.

Eluding the Coast Guard had become more and more difficult. In the winter of 1925–26, for the first time in its long and distinguished history, the Coast Guard experimented with keeping its patrol boats on the Great Lakes during the winter as a deterrent to anyone foolish enough to try smuggling. Their powerful six-bitters could battle their way through ice fields which sometimes covered hundreds of acres and floated barely visible on the lake. The Coast Guard never repeated the experiment.

During the months when Kerr operated the *Pollywog* alone, he made the long run from Hamilton to Belleville and then, after loading with Corby's whisky, travelled across the lake to Rochester. He would frequently leave Hamilton in the morning and not finish his day until 2 or 3 the next morning. Wesley Thomas, the lighthouse keeper at main Duck, commented, "not many of them would work alone on that lake." If the weather was not right, Ben would put in at Main Duck and visit with Wes and his wife, Ila, in their home adjacent to the lighthouse. Kerr would not make the run on a cloudless, moonlit night, but would stay over at Main Duck waiting for a dark or rainy night. The U.S. Coast Guard had become too much of a threat to risk crossing when the visibility was good.

Just how big a threat became obvious in the summer of 1926. The conflict between the Coast Guard and the bootlegging community had grown more and more violent. Threats were made against some of the coast guardsmen and even against their families. After threats were made on his life, Mason McCune, the captor of *Martimas* and Kerr, began carrying a .32 Savage automatic revolver – even when off duty. His brother, Merle McCune, who was based at Oswego, carried a .32 Colt automatic for the same reason. Merle was the officer usually in charge of picket boat *2207* and quickly racked up an exceptional record of captures. Paul Lobdell crewed on *2207* and recalls that they usually set out about ten in the evening and did not return until dawn. George Loomis, who also served under Merle McCune, remembers that their usual tactic was to crisscross back and forth all night, hoping to intercept a black ship. Both men remember Merle having an unusual ability to sense where the rumrunners might be headed. That was certainly the case on the night of 15 July 1926.

Leo Yott, a Syracuse bootlegger turned rumrunner, picked up a cargo of four hundred cases of O'Keefe beer in Deseronto from Mid "Shorty" Hunt on 10 July, giving his destination as Rochester. Shorty Hunt, who stood almost seven feet tall, operated a beer storage warehouse which was perfectly legal under Canadian law. Yott followed the proper procedure of having the B-13's completed. Canadian Customs authorities then phoned this information to American authorities who alerted the Coast Guard of Yott's departure in the fifty-two-foot cruiser *Andy*. To confuse the Coast Guard, Yott had given a false destination, and to throw them off his track still further, he spent a few days at Picton. Six days after clearing from Deseronto, Yott decided to chance a crossing. Around midnight, the *Andy* left Picton, heading in the direction of Fair Haven Bay, about 20 miles (32 km) west of Oswego. Merle McCune was cruising in that vicinity keeping an eye on a section of the beach suspected of being used as a drop by rumrunners. Merle's procedure was to stop periodically so that the crew could listen for the sound of a black ship's motor; many of these boats were equipped with underwater exhausts to muffle the sound of their engines, making them difficult to hear. About 2 a.m. they heard the muffled throb of the *Andy*. Picket boat *2207* was started and ran in the direction of the sound, the motor was cut, and the listening began again.

Eventually, they came across Andy's wake which they followed for about ten minutes before sighting the rumrunner. Merle instructed his crew, consisting of mechanic Bill Paeny and surfman George Loomis, to run abeam of the black ship, keeping the search light on her, and hailing them to "heave to." In his report McCune describes what followed:

No attention was paid to hails and a revolver was fired in the air also a rifle was emptied, but boat's speed was not slackened but headed for shore. Machine gun was then fired at intervals across bow with stops to permit surrender, and an attempt to run picket boat down was made, she then headed out into the lake as if to get into Canadian waters [about twenty miles or thirty-two kilometres north] she was followed with shots from machine gun, one magazine being emptied without hitting her, a second magazine was used and shots fired into bows, and port side, her speed was not checked and shots made into pilot house, 8 revolver, 6 rifle, and 93 machine gun shots were fired in all, when boat checked speed and lost all headway, a flash light was kept on pilot house all this time. A man came out of the wheel house with a light and said a man was hurt then another man came out. Both were ordered to put up hands and hand irons were put on them. Boarded boat and found a man apparently dead, examined hole [means hold] of boat but no others were aboard, hole was nearly full of bags of bottled beer ... 4 a.m. ... returned to boat with Doctor Griggs where he pronounced man dead.[7]

Leo Yott was the first rumrunner killed by the Coast Guard on the Great Lakes. Both Yott and his crew had long criminal records and so would not surrender readily. Moreover, Yott's cargo consisted of 9,600, 22 oz. bottles of O'Keefe's Ale, over 8 percent, which he had purchased for just twenty cents a bottle in Canada but which would bring him $1.25 each in his bootlegging territory of Syracuse. His gross profit on the load was therefore slightly over $10,000, and from this his expenses would be minimal.

Coast Guard officials had issued warnings on numerous occasions, declaring that they would fire on rum ships that refused to stop. Since much of public opinion in the United States was still sympathetic to the bootleggers, the smugglers didn't believe they would be fired upon. The shooting of Leo Yott changed all this. As George Jackson, the captain in charge of the Oswego Station reported:

> Reports are many that a gang of tough characters have made threats in Syracuse, that they are going to "get" members of this crew. It is regretted that it was necessary to use extreme measures to make seizure but it was evident that he did not intend to be taken and his death has made a lasting impression on others that have taken the Coast Guard lightly, thinking and saying we would not use the guns if they would not surrender.[8]

The stakes in the game of chase between rumrunner and Coast Guard had gone up. It was no longer, catch me if you can, but surrender or be shot. On Lake Ontario the new policy produced immediate results. In the two months following the shooting of Yott, there were four major captures of rum ships and their crews in eastern Lake Ontario. Two of these took place at the recently reopened station at Big Sandy, the other two at Oswego. The largest took place on 22 September, when Merle McCune arrested Captain Ferguson and his three man crew, and seized the fifty-nine ton schooner (53.5 tonnes), *Pinta*, carrying 2,400 quarts of beer hidden under a cargo of coal.

In spite of these successes, the Coast Guard was still more of an irritant than an impediment to the bootlegging community. While Oswego Station made several captures in the summer of 1926, the Rochester Coast Guard station managed only one for the entire year. It too involved the firing of guns into a black ship before its captain – the notorious Wild Bill Sheldon – surrendered. The boat he was commanding, the *Jim Lulu*, had been used by various smugglers for several years. It was a beautiful forty-five-foot cruiser estimated to be worth at least $8,000. But it was powered by one Peerless 50 hp motor, and could make no more than eight or nine knots (15 to 17 km/h). Like the *Martimas*, the *Jim Lulu* was simply too slow to be effective. This was true of almost all the boats employed by rumrunners up to about 1926. After that year, the successful smugglers either used very fast boats or, in a few cases, heavily armoured craft with firepower equal to that of the Coast Guard. Lacking the nerve and unwilling to risk the capital, a large number of smugglers did not adopt these tactics but relied on inexpensive boats crewed by others. By the fall of 1928, most of these operators had been driven out of the business.

Kerr clearly enjoyed the *Pollwog*'s reputation as the fastest boat on the lake. Bill Lynch, who worked at Corby's and helped load the *Pollywog* at the Belleville government docks, was still in awe of the memory when he recalled that Ben always took off at full speed, "you couldn't see his boat for the rooster tail, it looked like a giant sea gull."[9] Kerr needed the speed. The Coast Guard had him at the top of their most-wanted list and the United States government had offered a $5,000 reward for information leading to his capture. Kerr was easily the best known of the Canadian rumrunners. His defiant statements attracted attention as did his reputed wealth. As a result of his skipping out and forfeiting his bail bond, the U.S. Justice Department attempted to have him extradited to face charges of smuggling. However, these charges were not recognized as extraditable by the Canadian government. These failures only served to strengthen the resolve of American law officers to capture Kerr and bring him to justice.

During most of 1926, Ben operated *Pollywog* alone, buying beer from Montreal, Kitchener, and Toronto, from where it would be trucked to Belleville or Trenton. Once the *Pollywog* was loaded, he would leave promptly at four in the afternoon. Several old timers remember that, "you could set your watch by him." On the way to Main Duck Island, Kerr would break open the wooden whisky cases and transfer the bottles into burlap bags, leaving a trail of floating cases in the *Pollywog*'s wake. If he was just carrying beer he did not have to do this as their cardboard cartons did not float. Nevertheless, he followed the same procedure with beer, repacking it into burlap bags in order to fit in as many cases as possible.

As well as his trips out of Belleville and Trenton, Kerr was also making frequent crossings of Lake Ontario from Hamilton, taking loads of seventy-five to eighty cases of Gooderham and Worts whisky to an M. Wilkes of Olcott, New York, which is near Niagara Falls. Wilkes would not be the buyer's real name, but it is almost certain that a bootlegger in Olcott was the customer. These trips were much easier to make than the long runs from Hamilton to Belleville and then over to Rochester. Kerr could leave Hamilton and be at the Gooderham and Worts export docks at the foot of Trinity Street in about an hour. After loading, the trip to Olcott would take perhaps twenty minutes longer. On each case of whisky delivered, Kerr grossed seven dollars. A load of eighty cases yielded him $560 for a few hours work. At that time a new Ford Roadster cost about $800. Alf Wheat may have travelled with Kerr on some of the trips to Olcott and received from fifty to a hundred dollars per trip.

Cancelled cheques seized by the OPP reveal that, beginning in October of 1925, Ben Kerr was making extra profits on his return trips by smuggling raw alcohol back into Canada. This product was industrial alcohol produced legally by the distilleries in the United States for use in industry. In reality, a lot of this alcohol was shipped to pharmaceutical companies which then illegally removed the poisons which had made it unfit for human consumption. If done properly, the resultant product could be used to "make" whisky, gin, scotch, or whatever drink the creative bootlegger desired. Caramel was used to simulate the colour of scotch, a touch of fusel oil approximated the taste of whisky. Fusel oil is poisonous so care had to be taken not to add too much. Often the raw alcohol was simply mixed with water and used to dilute good whisky. Unfortunately for the bootleggers' customers, the raw alcohol was not always safe to drink. Methyl alcohol, also known as wood alcohol, was one of the chemicals added to drinking alcohol in order for it to qualify as industrial alcohol. This highly toxic alcohol is difficult to separate from ethyl – or drinking – alcohol. In very small quantities it is poisonous but not necessarily deadly. Fortunately for the imbiber, industrial alcohol contained only about 2 percent wood alcohol and therefore was not fatal unless a large amount was consumed. But a disaster occurred when one shipment of industrial alcohol turned out to be almost pure wood alcohol.

The horror began on the morning of 22 July 1926, in the little village of Allanburg. Three bachelors had purchased a one gallon tin of alcohol from a local bootlegger the previous day. Neighbours were attracted by the screams of the suffering men. Constable Reece called Doctor Herod who arrived at eight a.m. to find Reuben Upper and John MacDonald, "in a dying condition." Charles Durham, a teamster, was seriously ill but expected to survive.

MacDonald was pronounced dead at 9 a.m.; Upper died ten minutes later. Durham was taken to the Welland County hospital in St. Catharines were he died the next day in great agony. In the room where the men had been partying, Constable Reece found a half-empty tin of alcohol which was taken for analysis. The police noted that the tin was from the U.S.A. because the gallon size was smaller than the Canadian imperial gallon.

On 23 July at Oakville, George Gill, a retired farmer with a wife and three children, along with Tom Lyon and Jim Johnston, both bachelors, were found in great agony. All three died shortly afterwards. Chief David Kerr of Oakville made arrangements to have the can of alcohol found with them chemically analyzed. That same day in Hamilton, the tenant at 277 Barton Street returned home from work to find his boarder, Poill Sinka, violently ill and unable to stand or see. Doctor Porter arrived shortly thereafter but Sinka, hallucinating and screaming in agony, died within the hour. Hearing of Sinka's death, Chief Kerr phoned the Hamilton police station at 1 a.m. and spoke with detective Joe Crocker. The two policemen agreed to cooperate and compare the results of the analysis of the cans found with the victims. But by now the deaths had attracted the attention of the provincial government. On Saturday 24 July, the acting attorney general W.H. Price (the attorney general, William Nickle, was on holidays) brought together all departments of the government. The OPP, the Liquor License Board, the health ministry, and the attorney general's department all agreed to coordinate their efforts in an attempt to stop the deaths and trace the source of the poison. At Hamilton that same Saturday morning, Catharine Foreman of 228 Hess Street North was found in great agony by her friend, Mary Herman. She was rushed to hospital but died that afternoon. Mrs. Foreman had five children ranging in age from four months to ten years. Herman had four children herself but volunteered to temporarily take care of the deceased woman's children. Police tried to locate the husband who was reported to be in Kapuskasing but were unsuccessful. A few days later the children were turned over to the Children's Aid Society. It was expected that they would become wards of St. Mary's Orphans' Home.

Meanwhile, Chief Kerr had been busy. That same Saturday morning he arrested William Maybee, who operated a service station on the Dundas highway near Oakville. Kerr had determined that Maybee had sold the poison alcohol to Thomas Lyon, who had died on Friday. Kerr also arrested Maybee's wife and two grown sons. Maybee's wife admitted that her husband, who was handicapped, had been bootlegging for years to supplement their income. During the arrests, William Maybee became violently ill and had to be rushed to St. Michael's hospital in Toronto. He died in great agony that Saturday afternoon, a victim of the poison liquor he had been selling.

While Chief Kerr had been arresting Maybee in Oakville, Detective Crocker made what looked to be a major break through in the case when he arrested Bert D'Angelo who lived at 153 Ferris Street East in Hamilton. D'Angelo admitted selling two one-gallon tins of alcohol to George Gill that Tuesday in Oakville. He admitted he had another can of the stuff in his garage, and made a signed voluntary statement that the alcohol had been delivered to him by one Ed "Red"

Miller of 84 Tisdale Street North, who was an employee of Harry Sullivan, a well-known bootlegger.

Meanwhile the death toll continued to mount. On Monday, the *Hamilton Spectator* announced that, in the previous week, fifteen people had died in Ontario from poison alcohol. Five of the victims had died in Hamilton. In Buffalo, which was believed to be the source of the poison, the death toll had climbed to thirteen. That day, the OPP sent its most prominent and experienced investigators into action. General Williams, commissioner of the force, accompanied by James Hales KC, chairman of the Liquor Board, travelled to Hamilton, and then to Buffalo to confer with top legal and police officials there. Williams made the trip to emphasize the urgency of the case and to secure full cooperation from the local police forces in Hamilton, Oakville, St. Catharines, and Niagara Falls. Like the OPP, they were under the general administration of the attorney general's office. That department wanted them to know they were to cooperate fully with the OPP. There was to be no playing politics or protecting local relatives and friends who might happen to be bootleggers. Commissioner Williams also wanted to assure the Americans of his and the government's full cooperation. He was hoping they would make available to the OPP the information they had on those Canadians buying raw alcohol from the American distilling ring.

Two of the OPP's most experienced criminal investigators, William Stringer and Albert Moss, travelled to Hamilton on Monday 26 July to work with detective Joe Crocker of Hamilton. Moss returned later that day to follow up leads in Toronto. In Hamilton, the word on the street was that Rocco Perri had threatened that, "anyone who talked would be dealt with." But detective Crocker and Inspector Stringer were experienced and highly capable investigators. They interrogated Edward "Red" Miller for over an hour and extracted a statement from him implicating Joe Romeo who was known to work for Rocco Perri. The statement signed on 27 July, reads as follows:

> I am a single man age 20 years, living at my mother's home, 84 Tisdale Street North, Hamilton. I work for Harry Sullivan on Main Street East. About 2 weeks ago Harry Sullivan told me that Bert D'Angelo wanted 3 gallons of alcohol and told me to go and get it from Joe Romeo, 25 Railway Street, Hamilton. I made a trip and seen Bert D'Angelo and told him that I could not secure the alcohol just then. I then met Harry Sullivan on the same day and he told me to go to a garage that he

had rented and there get 3 cans of alcohol. I went there with my Ford and picked up 3 cans of alcohol at this garage. I took the 3 cans to Bert D'Angelo on Ferrie Street and delivered the alcohol to him personally. He paid me $33 for the alcohol. I then went over to 25 Railway Street and paid Mrs. Romeo $30 for the alcohol received by Harry Sullivan from Joe Romeo.[10]

Witnessed Joe Crocker
signed, Ed Miller

W.H. Stringer

All that was needed to tie Rocco Perri to the poison brew was to get Joe Romeo to admit he bought it from Perri. That afternoon, Crocker and Stringer arrested Joe Romeo and held both he and Miller on a charge of vagrancy. The biggest fish in the net was Joe Romeo, who lived at 499 Hughson Street. Romeo was known to have worked for Perri since 1923 when the rumrunner John Gogo had been shot and killed by Toronto police. Romeo was a hardened criminal who had been well coached by Perri. Romeo clammed up and refused to make any statement to the police. The analysis of the alcohol found at the death sites came in from Professor Rogers of the University of Toronto. It was found to be composed of 93 percent wood alcohol; just a small amount would cause blindness or death. Police Chief Kerr of Oakville noted that Jim Johnston, who he described as a decent chap and a distinguished war veteran, had died after just one drink of the stuff, and his brain had not one drop of blood in it, "so deadly is the poison."[11] A modern pathologist would add that methanol (or wood alcohol) first causes severe headaches, followed by convulsions, acidosis, collapse of the circulatory system, and respiratory failure. As little as 30 ml can cause death, and 250 ml is always fatal.

Obviously some people didn't read the newspapers or listen to the news on the radio because people were still drinking and dying from bootleg hootch. On Wednesday, 28 July, despite four days of poison liquor headlines, Irene Colesnik was added to the casuality lists. A mother of four young children, she lived in the Ward district of Toronto, a ghetto heavily populated with first-generation immigrants. It is possible that Colesnik did not read or understand English. The death toll in Ontario now stood at nineteen.

Both in Canada and the United States, the highest levels of government were now involved. Premier Ferguson, also known as "Foxy" Fergy, commented that the province's liquor policy might be affected. Ferguson was known to favour abolishing the OTA and replacing it with government-controlled liquor stores.

Sensing that the OTA was in danger, the head of the Dominion Alliance came out strongly against this option, stating that even before Prohibition, people had died from drinking poisonous alcohol, and that the OTA was not to blame for the deaths. He was correct in that occasionally someone did die from drinking bad hootch; usually homebrew prepared by someone with little or no knowledge of chemistry. But never before had there been deaths from alcohol poisoning on such large scale.

The investigation on the American side was achieving dramatic results. Prohibition agents struck near the top of the criminal organization when they arrested James Voelker on 27 July. Police had raided his residence, described by the press as a mansion, and seized much incriminating evidence, including cancelled cheques, bank deposits, and a long list of telephone calls. One of the most frequently phoned was Louis Sylvester, a Perri bootlegger in Thorold.

At this point, Inspector Stringer left Hamilton and travelled to Buffalo to learn what the Americans had found out that might assist the Canadian authorities. He discovered that while Voelker had not been helpful, the documents seized revealed a ring extending to New York City, Toronto, the Niagara Peninsula, and the Maritime provinces. Two drug companies were involved in the redistilling operation and the ring operated a fleet of boats and cars. The poison liquor had been shipped via freight train from New York City hidden under a pile of coal. Stringer learned that a raid had been made the previous May on the Third Ward Political Club which was part of the bootleggers' redistilling operation. A safe on the premises had been drilled and incriminating documents found. The American authorities were about to issue indictments against those Canadians listed in the documents as buyers of the denatured alcohol. The list included: Max Wortzman, Harry Goldstein, Fanny Shulman, Rocco Perri, J.B. Kerr, Harry Sullivan, John McRae, Jas. Sacco, John Tychynski, Frank Boyd, William Hebert, John Cerroni, and Louis Sylvester.

On 29 July, the United States attorney at Buffalo, Richard Templeton, announced ninety-one indictments as a result of the raids made in May against the Third Ward Political Club. All of the Canadians noted above were on the list of indictments. Acting Attorney General Price and OPP Commissioner Victor Williams then laid charges of manslaughter against all of the Canadians named by the Americans. This was done in spite of the fact that of those indicted by the Americans only a few could be connected to the poison liquor.

Shortly after 1 a.m. on the morning of 30 July 1926, Inspector Ward of the Criminal Investigations Branch of the OPP, accompanied by Detective Crocker of the Hamilton City Police, called at the residence of Ben Kerr, bearing a warrant for his arrest on charges of manslaughter and smuggling. Loudly protesting his innocence, Kerr was taken to the old Barton Street jail in Hamilton's north end. The next morning, he came before Magistrate Jeffs in the dingy police court on King William Street and was formally charged. His application for bail was denied.

Rocco Perri went missing for a day but surrendered to police the next morning. Meanwhile the Ontario Provincial Police, in cooperation with various city police forces, were rounding up suspects from Niagara Falls through to Toronto. Ben Kerr and Rocco Perri now found themselves at the centre of what was then the largest criminal investigation in the history of Canada.

An elegant Ben Kerr, pianist, posed for this photo in 1906.
Elli and George Urban

A streetcar heading back to the sheds after the mob had stoned out most of its windows during the street railway strike of 1906.

Photo courtesy of the Hamilton Public Library

Ben Kerr is seated on the left. His bride-to-be, Louisa Byrens, is seated on the right. Ben and Louisa are flanked by her seated parents. Kerr's older brother George is standing behind to the right. Circa 1911.

Elli and George Urban

E
X
P
E
R
I
E
N
C
E
D

H
O
N
E
S
T

YOURS IN SERVICE
GEORGE G.
HALCROW
AS
CONTROLLER

Six Years in The City Council

In December of 1925, George Halcrow ran for Hamilton controller and was narrowly defeated. Politically, it was his last hurrah.
Photo by Marion Raycraft

Kerr's rumrunner the Evelyn *in Trenton harbour. The man in the stern is "Gunner" Alf Wheat. Circa 1923.*

Elli and George Urban

The rumrunner Martimas *was captured by the U.S. Coast Guard after a shootout at Rochester in May of 1925. Kerr was captured with it.*

U.S. National Archives

The Pollywog *was one of the fastest rumrunners on Lake Ontario. Jack Morris Jr. is standing at the bow of the boat.*
Elli and George Urban

The Pollywog, *on the ice in Hamilton harbour during the winter of 1925-26. This photo was used to identify the wreckage found in the summer of 1994.*
Elli and George Urban

Ben Kerr, in the stern of his rumrunner the Voyageur. *Circa 1923.*
Elli and George Urban

Ben Kerr's marine storage lockers in 1925. They were torn down in the early 1970s. A modern marina sits on the site today.
Elli and George Urban

Rocco Perri in 1926 when he reluctantly testified before the Royal Commission on Customs and Excise.

Photo by the Hamilton Spectator

Entrance to one of the secret rooms where Kerr kept his contraband alcohol which he smuggled in from the U.S.A. for Rocco Perri. This is in back of the former Kerr home on Bay Street North in Hamilton.
Photo by author

A dapper Jack Morris (smuggler) flanked by two friends. Circa 1928.
Photo by Sandra Stokes

Boat builder Jack Morris Jr. helped build the speedy Pollywog. *He was one of the boat's three-man crew during the years it was used as a rumrunner. Circa 1930.*
Photo by Sandra Stokes

The Corby/Wiser distillery complex (as photographed in the early 1950s) of eighty buildings covered twenty-three acres. Located ten kilometres north of Belleville, it was a major supplier to Ben Kerr. It was torn down in the summer of 1995.

Photo by Ralph Plumpton

Inspector William Stringer of the CID division of the OPP is standing on the left. Stringer and two detectives went to Windsor to bring back a suspect in the poison liquor deaths.

Ontario Archives

Kerr sponsored the Pals hockey team. He is the tall man in the fur coat and Arundel fedora standing on the right. Kelly Thompson, coach of the team, is in the cameo. Circa 1923.
Photo by Kelly Thompson

Ben Kerr, in fur coat and Arundel fedora, standing with members of the Pals hockey team. Circa 1923.
Photo by Kelly Thompson

Presqu'ile Bay Harbour where Kerr loaded the Pollywog *with gas and whisky before heading across the lake. This area is now part of a provincial park.*
Photo by Purtell Quick

The cottage in the foreground was used by Kerr and Wheat as the jumping-off point for their smuggling operation into the U.S.A.
Photo by Purtell Quick

In the winter of 1928–29, Ben Kerr utilized the Presqu'ile Hotel's baby grand piano for his musical enjoyment.
Ontario Ministry of Natural Resources

Pilot Walter Leavens and his Eagle Rock aircraft used to search for Wheat and Kerr over Main Duck Island and the eastern end of Lake Ontario.
Photo by Ken Leavens

The damaged prop of the Pollywog, *discovered along with other wreckage in the summer of 1994 near Colborne by Tim Rawn and Tom Nelson.*
Photo by Michiel Duinker

Diver Michiel Duinker stands near the tall wooden cross overlooking the wreckage of the Pollywog *at McGlennon's point near Colborne.*
Photo by author

Thirteen

Cross-Border Crime

America's Prohibition law allowed their distilleries to manufacture denatured alcohol in limited quantities. It was used for a variety of purposes including perfumes, aftershave lotion, rubbing alcohol, and in a number of manufacturing processes. To qualify as denatured alcohol the government required that it be rendered poisonous by the addition of certain toxins. U.S. Federal regulations approved six formulas for completely denatured alcohol. They involved the addition to ethyl alcohol, (the chemical name for beverage alcohol), of small amounts of methyl alcohol (wood alcohol), kerosene, and formaldehyde. All of these chemicals are deadly poisons. Bootleggers would buy this alcohol and then "cook" it to remove the poisons. Methyl alcohol is extremely difficult to separate from ethyl alcohol and the bootleggers, most of whom lacked chemical knowledge, had limited success. An underground industry sprang up printing false labels for the bootleggers to put on the bottles in order to convince the consumer that the exorbitant price he was paying was for aged whisky produced in Canadian or Scottish distilleries. These labels were often so good that only an expert could tell them from the real thing. Bootleggers then sold this product to an unsuspecting public who, unwittingly, were slowly poisoning themselves.

American authorities knew that this practice was going on, partly because the number of deaths caused by poison liquor steadily increased during the years of Prohibition. As Canadian distilleries and breweries were allowed to manufacture beverage alcohol, there seemed to be no practical reason for this type of alcohol to be smuggled into Canada. But the police had not counted on the ingenuity nor on the immense greed of the bootleggers. In 1923, the Ontario Provincial Police seized their first load of distilled industrial alcohol, also called raw alcohol. Commissioner Williams noted that there is a need for, "a new point of view ... as it has become apparent that alcohol in very considerable quantities is being shipped into this Province from the United States, one shipment of as much as 500 gallons having being seized."[1]

The origin of this dangerous beverage was just across the Niagara River in New York State. At Buffalo, the Jopp Drug Company had been set up in 1922, ostensibly to manufacture toilet water. As this product required the use of denatured alcohol, the company was licensed to buy it from American distilleries. Raw alcohol is quite inexpensive to manufacture; it is the aging and blending of whisky which makes it expensive. The Jopp Drug Company could buy denatured alcohol for just $1.10 a gallon.

A few kilometres away in Niagara Falls, Joseph Sottile and his brother-in-law, Joe Spallino, had set up the Falls Tonic Manufacturing Company for exactly the same purpose. Both companies purchased denatured alcohol under license from the federal government. It was then moved to the secret plant operated by Sottile and his brother-in-law, where it was "cooked" to remove the poisons. In order to do this they had to have the connivance of at least some police officials plus a well disguised plant to do the redistilling. Sottile and Spallino had their offices in the Third Ward Political Club at 13th Street in Niagara Falls. Their offices were linked by a tunnel to their redistilling plant which was hidden away in the abandoned National Theatre located next door. The plant had several thousand gallons of manufacturing and storage capacity and was quite sophisticated. Well educated himself, Sottile hired legitimate chemists to test his product in an effort to ensure that it was reasonably safe to drink.

Both the Jopp Drug Company and the Falls Tonic Company were in full production by the summer of 1923, supplying alcohol to a number of Canadian and American bootlegging gangs. Perri was a major player in the distribution of this alcohol into Canada. He supplied Sottile with Canadian liquor and beer in return for raw alcohol and cash. In February of 1924, both Kerr and Perri appear in Sottile's books as large individual buyers. At this point, Kerr was acting independently, but in the summer of 1925, he was forced into becoming a mere transporter of the product for Rocco Perri. Perri controlled bootlegging in the Hamilton region and had the organization to distribute the alcohol. Moreover, Perri had made an arrangement with Gooderham and Worts in the spring of 1925 requiring Perri's approval for any purchases made by Kerr from that distillery. As Kerr was purchasing whisky from Gooderham and Worts during the fall of 1925, he must have agreed to Perri's terms. He bought Canadian liquor and sold it to Americans designated by Rocco, who no doubt took a cut on these transactions. As Insp. William Stringer noted, the criminal organizations were composed of rings within rings.

John Kerr, a nephew of Ben, remembers that Ben's two younger brothers, Gordon and Ernest, often kept watch for the Hamilton police from the top of the hill on Bay Street, which overlooks the harbour and Kerr's marine garage. If the police were in the area, the brothers would signal Kerr, who would be out in the harbour waiting for the all-clear signal before coming in. As Kerr's arrangement with Perri prevented him from smuggling booze back into Canada, he was almost certainly smuggling American raw alcohol. Once in his marina, he could stash the alcohol in one of the three secret rooms he had built into the hill at the back of his garage. Perri's men would later pick it up and distribute it. Rocco never touched these jobs himself, making it extremely difficult for the police to arrest him. Those who might have testified against Perri had a discouraging tendency to leave the country or disappear altogether.

The American criminal Sottile was as clever as Perri and certainly more dangerous. American police believed Sottile to be the head of the Black Hand Society, forerunner to the modern-day Mafia. After meeting with officials of the U.S. Bureau of Investigation, later to become the FBI, Inspector Stringer of the OPP reported to Commissioner Williams that Sottile was responsible for the bombing murder of undercover agent Orville Preuster. Preuster had done much to stop the flow of alcohol across the border into Canada. Sottile was also suspected in the attempts to murder two Niagara Falls church ministers who had carried on a vigorous campaign against the vice and corruption in western New York.

Sottile and James Lavallée of New Brunswick, who was one of that province's most enterprising booze merchants, were the masterminds who concocted the brilliant scheme to smuggle raw alcohol into Canada, transport it to the island of St. Pierre and Miquelon, and there mix it with expensive brands of Scottish whisky. With the use of counterfeit labels, the resulting product could then be sold for top dollar to the bootleg gangs in Boston and New York. Believing they were buying genuine Scotch and Canadian whisky, these gangs would then cut the doctored product still further in order to maximize their own profits.

The drinking public in America had come to realize that much of the bootleg booze they were drinking had been manufactured under conditions that were unsanitary at best, and at worst, downright dangerous and life threatening. The term "bathtub gin" originates from Prohibition and refers to the concoctions which were manufactured in the tenement buildings under the direction of organized criminals.

These buildings were generally infested with rats and cockroaches. Not infrequently, these unwanted additions found their way into the mash, adding a certain "body" to the mixture. When the Chicago police raided one of these places, they found dead rats in each of the one hundred barrels of mash they confiscated. Consequently, top-quality Scotch, arriving in large ships from Europe and sold in the waters off New York and Boston, commanded the very highest price since it was believed to be pure and undiluted.

In the summer of 1925, Sottile travelled to the French island of St. Pierre and Miquelon for a meeting with James Lavallée who owned the *Ruth*, an ocean going vessel, which he used to carry high quality Scotch from St. Pierre and Miquelon to rum row where it was sold to any bootlegger with the money to buy it. The Scotch, was considered to be of the best quality as it was presumed to have come directly from the ancient distilleries of that proud whisky-making race. One of the earliest rumrunners to use St. Pierre and Miquelon as a transshipping point had been Bill McCoy. The popular expression, "it's the real McCoy" had originated from the belief that his whisky had came directly from Scotland and was therefore the genuine article. As a consequence, bootleggers paid a premium price for whisky purchased off rum row from large ocean-going ships. But the *Ruth* did not cross the Atlantic. Lavallée loaded it from booze already stockpiled on the island. It was an easy matter to dilute the good Scotch with alcohol from Sottile's Niagara Falls plant and sell it to the unsuspecting bootleggers off rum row as the "Real McCoy." The alcohol cost Sottile a dollar and ten cents a gallon. In a satanic version of the miracle of the loaves and fishes, one thousand cases of expensive Scotch could be magically transformed into two thousand or more cases at a minimal cost. Sottile and Lavallée were well on their way to making a fortune. In his later testimony to the Royal Commission on Customs and Excise, Lavallée admitted that they had grossed $184,000 on just one transaction.

This ingenious plan was brought to a halt by American Prohibition forces. On 14 May 1926, Mark Crehan led a special squad of Prohibition agents in a raid on the Third Ward Political Club where they seized the redistilling equipment, five thousand gallons of whisky, and twelve thousand gallons of alcohol, and arrested Joe Spallino, Sottile's brother-in-law and right-hand man. Sottile was nowhere to be found. Two days later, agent Crehan returned and drilled the safe in Spallino's office. The chequebooks, cancelled cheques, and ledgers which were found inside the safe incriminated a large number of

Canadians and Americans in the alcohol scheme. Police forces on both sides of the border had previously minimized the extent of organized crime. These documents helped to convince them of its extent and influence. It was estimated that the gang involved in the alcohol business in the Toronto-Buffalo area had assets totalling at least $15 million.[2]

The raid on the Third Ward Political Club had results which could not have been foreseen. By putting the largest supplier of raw alcohol in northern New York out of business, the Prohibition agents had created an acute demand for the product both in Ontario and in northern New York. In the absence of Joe Sottile, who was hiding out in the Maritimes, James Voelker, a Buffalo bootlegger who worked for the shadowy crime lord Don Simone and who was allied with Sottile, contacted Davey Burden in New York City and demanded that raw alcohol be shipped as quickly as possible. Burden shipped twenty sixty-gallon drums to Voelker, who then sent eight cans to be tested by the chemists. In the meantime, he shipped out two of the sixty-gallon drums to Canada, releasing the rest to Buffalo bootleggers. The chemists tests showed that Voelker had shipped out deadly poison. It was not denatured ethyl alcohol which Voelker had shipped out, but highly poisonous wood alcohol to which had been added such toxins as acetone, formic acid, and formaldehyde. No amount of redistilling could have rendered this concoction harmless. It is not known if Voelker knew the alcohol was poisonous before he released it, but he made no effort to inform his buyers afterwards, who went about selling it to an unsuspecting public. The first painful deaths began just two days after Voelker shipped the drums to Ontario.

In the meantime, Sottile had fled. First to Toronto, where Perri took him to Max and Harry Wortzman. The year before, Sottile had made an application for Canadian citizenship but it had been held up by a report from RCMP Sgt. Frederick Lewis, who stated that he suspected Sottile was preparing to go into the rumrunning business in New Brunswick. But Sottile had connections in the Liberal Party in Ottawa. On 8 June, Sottile went before Judge Emerson Coatsworth in Toronto and requested a special hearing on his citizenship application. The hearing was granted. The next day the U.S. attorney in Buffalo issued a warrant for Sottile's arrest. As was standard practice, the Canadian Immigration Department was notified. Nevertheless, eight days after his hearing on 8 June, Sottile received his Canadian citizenship. Sottile then travelled to Saint John, New Brunswick, where he stayed with James Lavallée.

Meanwhile immigration officials, now aware that Sottile was likely involved in criminal activities, ordered him arrested and deported on the grounds that he was in Canada illegally. At his deportation hearing in Saint John, Sottile had merely to show his newly granted citizenship papers to secure his release.

At Ottawa, the immigration department began to press for the cancellation of Sottile's naturalization on the grounds of criminal activity and the false statements which he had made in his application; the most blatant being that he claimed to have been in Canada for five years when it had been only a few weeks. But Undersecretary of State Thomas Mulvey held that there was insufficient grounds to revoke his citizenship. Once again Sottile's friends in the Liberal Party had intervened on his behalf. With his safety in Canada seemingly assured, Sottile headed back to Niagara Falls to try and salvage his redistilling operation.

It had been Sottile and Don Simone who had given Voelker the approval to release the alcohol received from Davey Burden in New York before they had received the chemist's results. Greed had overtaken caution with disastrous results. Less than two weeks after its release, some forty-one people in Ontario and northern New York had died painfully from Burden's poisonous alcohol. On 29 July, Sottile, Voelker, and all those whose names appeared on the books of the Third Ward Political club, including many Canadians, were charged with violations of the Volstead Act. By the time the Americans had filed their indictments, the canny Sottile had already fled to Canada and was on his way back to Saint John.

On 30 July, William Nickle, Ontario's attorney general, issued warrants for the arrest of those Canadians previously indicted in New York. Unlike the American indictments which merely alleged violations of the Volstead Act, the Canadian indictments were for the much more serious offence of manslaughter. Although there was virtually no evidence connecting Rocco Perri, Ben Kerr, Max Wortzman or the other Canadians with the poison liquor deaths, the work of a Pinkerton man hired by the Ontario Government had convinced the Attorney General that a connection could be found. The Pinkerton man had gone undercover in the Hamilton-Niagara region. He spoke fluent Italian and was apparently attractive to women. Mildred Stirling, a woman with extensive underworld connections, who claimed she was known as the "Queen of the Bootleggers," became enamoured of the Pinkerton man and shed some light on Perri's position in the underworld and his connections to the poison liquor. Stirling had driven many a load of booze into the U.S. both by auto and by boat. The Pinkerton man, who sent in his reports under the initials J.C.S., spoke to a number of minor criminals several of whom connected Perri to the poison booze. In one conversation with Stirling, she is reported to have stated:

> Rocco Perri and his strong arm men have the town (Hamilton) scared to death and those fellows (poison liquor survivors), who narrowly escaped death are afraid, more now (since Perri's arrest) than ever before ... Over here you see, we have a magistrate Jeff, and he is a bad one, but not with the higher ups. Rocco Perri has this fellow tied around his little finger. Rocco can get anything done. All he has to do is flash the high ball (meaning a signal of some kind) and the works are in; that is why Rocco has been getting away with lots of trouble. Another thing, Bessie, a Jewish woman, who is Rocco's wife, is the brains of the works, and also has plenty of money. She gave him his start and today he is a millionaire.[3]

Unfortunately for the cause of justice in Ontario, the reports of the Pinkerton operative consisted solely of hearsay evidence which was, and still is, inadmissible in a court of law. Attorney General "Billy" Nickle issued the warrants to arrest Perri and the others in the hope that top OPP criminal investigators would uncover enough evidence to connect him to the poison liquor shipment. Nickle also expected that the information uncovered by American Prohibition and police forces would strengthen his case against the bootleg king and his associates. The Pinkerton agent's reports had pointed to Joseph Sottile as the man behind the distribution of the poison alcohol in Ontario. Nickle therefore issued a $2,000 reward for Sottile's arrest.

Shortly after the arrest of Kerr and Perri, the Conservative prime minister of Canada, Arthur Meighen, appointed Peter White as special Crown counsel in the smuggling cases. A few days later, on 4 August, White laid additional charges against all suspects, including Perri and Kerr, for customs violations. Not to be upstaged, the Ontario attorney general's department then appointed McGregor Young as a special prosecutor in the manslaughter cases.

In the meantime, the RCMP were tracking Sottile who was hiding out in Halifax with George and Jim Monolopolis, two Greek brothers who used their restaurant, the Sea Grill, on Hollis Street near the waterfront, as a cover for their bootlegging operations. The Mounties traced Sottile to Halifax by intercepting his mail but were unable to locate him there despite extensive surveillance. The Monolopolis brothers had arranged for one of their bootlegging connections to rent a house for Sottile on posh South Park Street. Unfortunately, the Mounties were concentrating their surveillance efforts on the cheap boarding house districts where criminals on the run normally hid out.

Sottile's connections to the Mafia are made clear by the letters intercepted by the RCMP. They reveal that he was relying on the Mafia organization in Italy, normally used to smuggle aliens out, to get him back into his native country. After some delay, the Mafia obtained papers and a new identity for him as an Italian citizen named Giuseppe Faillia. Sottile's luck held. A short time before the Mounties figured out where he was staying and raided his hide out, Sottile boarded a train in Halifax. The well connected criminal went directly to Montreal where his political friends had arranged an Italian passport in the name of Faillia. In Montreal, he boarded the White Star liner, SS *Regina* bound for Liverpool, England. Police in Liverpool were notified by the Mounties and a description of Sottile was forwarded. Chief Detective Inspector Moore and a Sergeant Sullivan of the Liverpool Police interrogated Sottile, who had an abundance of documents to prove his false identity. Moreover, Sottile had lost about eighty pounds and did not resemble the description forwarded by the Mounties. Well groomed and articulate, Sottile was able to convince the two detectives that he was indeed Faillia, an innocent travelling salesman. He was released and made his way to Palermo, Italy.[4] The Mounties' best efforts had been thwarted by corrupt politicians and two credulous British policemen.

In Ontario, the Crown's attempt to make a case against its suspects was meeting with scant success. It could be shown that Bert D'Angelo had sold some of the poison liquor, resulting in the deaths of two men. It could also be shown that Edward "Red" Miller had delivered some of it. But these men were small fry, bit players in a major crime. To make a case against the larger fish, Attorney General Nickle needed the evidence held by the New York authorities. As their own case was falling apart, the Americans were reluctant to release their evidence to the Canadians.

On 7 August, a week after their arrests, Ben Kerr, Rocco Perri, Edward Miller, Harry Sullivan, and Joe Romeo came before Magistrate Jeffs. Their request for bail was denied and their cases remanded for one week. M.J. O'Reilly, a leading Liberal, acted for Perri, but Ben Kerr was unrepresented and spoke on his own behalf, asking if any charges other than manslaughter had been laid against him? When Magistrate Jeffs answered in the affirmative, pointing out that they were being charged with breaches of the customs act, Kerr proceeded to address the manslaughter charge as follows:

> I would like to state that I have never in my life tasted, sold, carted, bought, or had in my possession at any time any kind of alcohol. In spite of this, I was thrown into prison and have been there more than a week, during which time they have done everything in their power to find information to use against me. They have gone to my plant, torn up floors in my house and office, dug up my lawn, and been there day and night and have not found one solitary bit of evidence. I think that one week of this sort of thing is plenty. I should at least be allowed to go home on bail.[5]

The Crown attorney intervened pointing out that some very valuable evidence had in fact been found in the search of Kerr's home. Magistrate Jeffs pointed out that if he had been wrongfully cast into jail, he would have legal redress. "But what about the meantime?" the prisoner demanded. "Oh, in the meantime Mr. Kerr," replied the elderly magistrate, "you are remanded in custody for one week."[6] Magistrate Jeffs had seen through Kerr's theatrical performance and was unimpressed.

The valuable evidence referred to by the Crown attorney consisted of fifteen cancelled cheques, drawn on Kerr's bank account with the Bank of Hamilton at James and Barton Streets. They were usually in amounts between $2,000 and $2,500, and were payable to James Voelker or Joe Webber of Buffalo. The Crown naturally assumed that these cheques were in payment for raw alcohol, but Kerr was able to show that they matched the amounts and dates of shipments of whisky which he had picked up from Gooderham and Worts. After examining the evidence and checking with the distillery, Inspector Stringer of the OPP was forced to conclude that Kerr's explanation held up. Kerr was no doubt telling the truth about the cheques, but this does not explain why he was listed on the books of the Third Ward Political Club as one of their major customers of raw alcohol. This was the evidence the OPP wanted, but which the Americans were reluctant to provide. However, it is unlikely even that evidence would have been enough. For a charge of manslaughter to stick the Crown attorney would at least have had to prove that Kerr had smuggled in the load of booze that caused the deaths.

At the next week's hearing, the Crown was unable to proceed but was still requesting that the accused be denied release on bail. The case against bail was argued by Crown Attorney George W. Ballard and by Special Prosecutor Percy White, of the federal customs branch, who argued that bail should not be granted because of the international nature of the case. O'Reilly, who again appeared for Perri, deferred to Kerr's lawyer, the distinguished Col. R.H. Greer KC of Toronto, who quoted at length from the Magna Carta. After an hour's discussion, Magistrate Jeffs ruled that he could no longer refuse bail, particularly in view of the fact that the Crown, when asked, declined to say when they would be ready to go ahead with the prosecution. Bail was set at the then considerable sum of $20,000. Both Perri and Kerr had no difficulty in making bail. They were ordered by Magistrate Jeffs to appear in court the following Saturday at which time the Crown might be ready to proceed.

The defendants appeared weekly for the next three weeks but each time the Crown was not ready to proceed with the trial. Finally, on 28 August, Magistrate Jeffs asked the Crown when they would be ready. Ballard answered that he did not know, but requested that the cases be adjourned week by week. Jeffs, who favoured dismissing the charges altogether, agreed that the case would be remanded week by week until the Crown was ready to proceed. He further ruled that the defendants need not appear unless the Crown notified them in advance that it was ready. Each week the courtroom had been crowded with spectators who strained to catch a glimpse of the suave Perri and the fulminating Kerr.

Now, it was clear, the spectators would have to come to court each week or risk missing the show. The disappointed crowd pushed its way out of the crowded courtroom as the prisoners exited. Beaming broadly, Rocco was met by Bessie who gave him a hug. "I guess they don't want us any more," smiled Rocco. "Looks like it," replied one of his mobsters.[7]

Behind all the publicity, the OPP was digging hard to put together a case. On 20 September, Attorney General Nickle travelled to Washington with Richard Templeton, the U.S. attorney at Buffalo, to meet with officials of the U.S. Justice Department. Nickle carried a nine-page report, prepared by Inspector Stringer of the CID, which summarized the findings of the OPP investigation. The report tied

Perri to the poison liquor deaths but only indirectly. Bert D'Angelo, who had sold the liquor to one of the victims, had given a statement naming Joe Romeo as the wholesale distributor of the stuff in the Hamilton area. Romeo had no visible means of support yet was the owner of a Big Six Studebaker, a touring model favoured by rum-runners and bootleggers because of its speed. He lived in a middle-class home on Hughson Street in Hamilton, and was known to be a member of the Perri gang ever since the shooting of John Gogo in Toronto. Unfortunately, none of this could be used to tie Perri direct-ly to the poison liquor and its distribution.

While in Washington, Nickle and Templeton met with President Calvin Coolidge, who had taken a personal interest in the case. As a result of the poison liquor deaths in the Buffalo area, the president had been deluged with letters, protesting against the addition of poisons to industrial alcohol. In response to these letters and the mounting toll of deaths from bad liquor, on 13 August 1926, the president ordered the cessation of the practice of adding wood alcohol to industrial alcohol.

Shortly after Nickle's return, the ubiquitous Inspector Stringer travelled to Windsor with Chief David Kerr of Oakville to locate the two Maybee brothers whose father had died from the poison liquor he had been selling. The two police officers located the two men in Detroit on 8 October, and persuaded them to return to Canada and give statements in the case against Edward "Red" Miller. Miller had earlier admitted delivering the bad liquor to Bert D'Angelo. The attorney general's department now felt that they had enough evi-dence to proceed to trial against D'Angelo. On 18 November, a jury found the fruit peddler guilty of manslaughter and he was sentenced to four years.

The province was now in the midst of a provincial election, called by Premier Howard Ferguson on 19 October, and to be held on 1 December 1926. Ferguson was offering government controlled liquor sales to replace the Ontario Temperance Act. The anti-liquor forces were enraged, and the resulting election campaign was one of the bit-terest in the province's history. One of the arguments used by Fergu-son was the need to get rid of the bootleggers and avoid any repeti-tion of the mass poisonings of the past summer.

Three days after the election, Magistrate Jeffs made a final ruling on the pending manslaughter cases against Perri and Kerr. Advised by the government's attorney, Gregory Young, that they were unable to proceed because certain witnesses in the United States were not available to testify, Jeffs ruled as follows:

I think these men are fairly entitled now to have it said that you are not going to proceed against them before me. They are tied up by the heavy bail imposed and are practically in the position of slaves … I will adjourn the customs charge for one week. The manslaughter charges are dismissed.[8]

The total collapse of the government's case against Kerr and Perri resulted from the decision by Premier Howard Ferguson to call an election on the issue of the OTA. When he did so, his Attorney General Nickle resigned his portfolio and was replaced by W.H. Price, a man that U.S. Attorney Richard Templeton, regarded as a wet and therefore not to be trusted. Consequently, Templeton refused to give photocopies of the books seized at the Third Ward Political Club to the Canadians.

It was the evidence needed to convict Perri and Kerr, if not of manslaughter then at least on the pending smuggling charges. In the United States, charges were dropped against all but James Voelker. On 21 December 1926, the man who had released the poison on an unsuspecting public, was convicted of manslaughter and sentenced to a term of fifteen to thirty years at Auburn Penitentiary.[9]

In Ontario, small-time bootlegger Bert D'Angello had appealed his conviction for manslaughter. After spending sixteen months in jail, Judge J.A. Ferguson overturned D'Angello's conviction, citing U.S. cases where there had been "no intent" to injure the victim. D'Angello was freed on 17 November 1927. He emerged into a province where the provincial government had replaced the bootlegger as the supplier of booze to its citizens.

For Perri, the poison liquor deaths had a critical impact on his criminal operations. The break up of the redistilling ring in Niagara Falls had eliminated his source of supply for industrial alcohol and destroyed the plan to dilute imported booze at the island of Saint Pierre and Miquelon. This was a major financial set back. But the ending of the OTA was an even greater set back, directly affecting his large Ontario bootlegging operation.

Fourteen

Bootleggers, Politicians, and Clergymen

I might be pardoned for referring to the result of the voting in divisions where bootleggers are said to congregate. It was freely said that they were voting for me, and nothing I could say seemed to dissipate such impression.

W.M. Brandon, defeated prohibitionist, candidate for Hamilton East, 2 Dec. 1926[1]

The poison liquor deaths that occurred during the summer of 1926 helped Premier Howard Ferguson bring an end to Prohibition in Ontario. But the premier's mind had been made up long before. The end of the OTA had been predicted in 1923 when the Conservatives had defeated the incompetent farmers' government of Ernest Drury. But Ferguson had been reluctant to proceed without first obtaining the people's approval. Accordingly, he called for a plebiscite on the OTA to be held on 23 October 1924.

The premier fully expected the people of Ontario to reject the OTA which had been a boon to bootlegging and had led to the growth of organized crime in the province. In place of the OTA, Ferguson expected a majority to vote for local option and government controlled liquor stores. Under this system, a town or city would hold a vote to decide if the majority desired a government store which could sell packaged liquor under strict controls. Alberta and British Columbia had recently voted for government controlled liquor sales, and just that summer, the province of Saskatchewan had voted overwhelmingly to replace its Prohibition law with a system of government controlled liquor stores. In spite of this trend, the premier was taking a risk. In the five plebiscites held on the question since 1894, the rural and Protestant community in Ontario had prevailed, and the province had voted dry by large margins. The most recent vote, taken in 1920, had stopped the importation of liquor into the province and so ended the mail order business which had been the middle classes' chief source of supply. Ferguson calculated that the professional and business classes, as a result of losing their home supply, had now soured on the OTA. No one wanted a return to the open bar and all its abuses, but many would vote for a man (or even a woman) being able to enjoy a drink in the privacy of their own home.

The churches, rural organizations, Women's Christian Temperance Association, the Dominion Alliance, and many other temperance organizations had been deeply suspicious of Ferguson and the Conservative Party when they had taken power from the United Farmers of Ontario. Ferguson was suspected of being a "wet" in sentiment. As a high-spirited student at the university of Toronto he had been the roommate of Canada's best known humorist and temperance critic, Stephen Leacock. As a professor of economics at McGill University, Leacock had no trouble buying liquor legally in wet Quebec. But when he returned to his summer home in Orillia, he could only get a bottle of good Scotch or rye by indulging in the fiction that he was ill. His doctor would then give him a prescription for a bottle of liquor which his local pharmacist would fill. The trick was to make sure your doctor was not a temperance man. Apparently a good portion of them were not, because the government sold about $5 million worth of liquor annually through drug stores. At that time an imperial quart bottle of Seagram's VO sold for $3, but a quart of Walker's Old Rye could be had for just $2. Three dollars and seventy five cents would buy a quart of the most expensive scotch available through the government dispensary. Writing prescriptions for liquor was so profitable that it came to constitute the largest part of some doctor's practices. To curb the abuses, the UFO government of Ernest Drury passed regulations limiting to fifty the number of liquor prescriptions any one doctor could write in a month. This reduced but did not stop the abuses.

In the legislative session of 1923, Attorney General Raney was attacked by the opposition for revealing the names of certain doctors who had abused their powers to write prescriptions. In typical fashion, the fanatical Raney responded by attacking Dr. Forbes Godfrey, the Conservative Member for York West. The attorney general pointed out that Doctor Godfrey had issued an average of 143 prescriptions for liquor per month until the government's decision to limit "script" to fifty a month. Doctor Godfrey's liquor prescriptions immediately fell to an average of just eighty-one per month. "What a rapid improvement in health there must have been in Mimico," dryly commented Raney.[2]

Ontario's attorney general was no respecter of the medical profession. In 1921, he was instrumental in removing the right to dispense liquor from 311 physicians. The next year, there was a drop in the issuance of script to a new low of 492,649. But this was a temporary trend. With Raney gone after 1923, the number of prescriptions for liquor began rising steadily. By 1924, they had risen to 724,920 for a total value of $5,028,747 which, in today's dollars, would approximate a hundred million a year.

Nor were physicians the only abusers. W.C.A. Moffatt, editor of the Druggists' Weekly, wrote in the Financial Post, "one of the most difficult problems facing the profession at the beginning of 1924 is ... the bootlegger who is carrying on his nefarious trade under the cloak of pharmacy. Of late the number of these so-called druggists has increased to ... an alarming extent."[3] The license inspectors agreed, and during the year, a number of raids were made on drugstores, checking the extent of their supplies, and verifying that the druggist had only been selling to people with valid prescriptions from their doctor. The government passed more regulations, limiting the amount of liquor a pharmacy could keep in stock, and restricting the size of the bottle that could be sold to just six ounces. The problem was checked somewhat, but those druggists determined to profit from the OTA continued to do so.

Court Miller, a retired pharmacist, recalls that he started in the profession in the last year of Prohibition, working for Bond's Drug Store in Peterborough. Like most druggists, J.P. Bond sold whisky legally to customers who brought in a prescription from their doctor. But he also took pure alcohol, and just like any gangster-bootlegger, cut it with water and then coloured it to look like real whisky. This he sold to customers who lacked a doctor's prescription. Miller thinks he might even have sold the counterfeit stuff to legitimate prescription customers. Bond made a great deal of money, but it did not buy him the respect of his associates. Miller held Bond in contempt. "He couldn't be trusted," says Miller, "it's a good thing Prohibition ended."[4]

By 1924, the medical profession was generally dissatisfied with its role as the medium for bringing liquor to the people of Ontario. That June at its annual convention in Ottawa, the Ontario Medical Association very nearly passed a resolution whereby physicians would refuse to be the government's liquor dispensers.

Dissatisfaction did not appear quite so openly among Ontario veterinarians. But widespread abuse of the liquor regulations existed

among certain veterinarians and there was a great deal of dissatisfaction with the OTA. D.H. Ackerill, a veterinarian practising in
Belleville, wrote to the editor of the *Daily Intelligencer* setting out the
arguments for the honest vet against the OTA. Ackerill pointed out
that, as a veterinary doctor, he could buy raw alcohol for just $2.60 a
gallon, and by adding two parts water to reduce it to normal beverage strength, his cost per gallon was reduced to just eighty-seven
cents. He could add a little colouring, pour it into quart bottles that
cost him fifteen cents each, and then sell each quart for five dollars.
His cost per quart was no more than forty cents, for a profit of $4.60
per quart. A vet was allowed to carry a quart of whisky with him
while making his rounds, presumably on the grounds that a horse
suffering heart problems needed that much to get its heart going. If
stopped by the police, the vet could always claim that the liquor he
carried was part of his job. As a consequence, it was very difficult to
prove a vet was bootlegging. Ackerill claimed that he and the other
two honest vets in the area were losing business to those vets who
sold booze to their clients. "He knows and realizes," he wrote, "that
many of [our] customers are slipping away causing he who is obeying the law to become hard up when the bootlegging vet who breaks
the law daily has lots of money to sport on and have a good time
always. Pretty galling don't you think, and a poor reward for [our]
faithfulness in keeping the law. IS THIS NOT PUTTING A PREMI-
UM ON CRIME WITH A VENGEANCE!"[5]

Premier Ferguson was relying on this sort of middle-class frus-
tration with the OTA, to help override the opposition of the majority
of the Protestant clergy, and in particular, the Methodists who were
the most inflexible in their opposition to any relaxing of Prohibition.
The Methodist Church was strongest in the farm communities, where
it reinforced the rural values of frugality, hard work, and abstinence.
To win the plebiscite, the wets would have to carry the cities and
towns by large majorities. Operating under the name of the Moderation League, the wet campaign was well organized and financed. The
drys, on the other hand, were slow to get started. The former farmer
government of Ernest Drury had passed all the laws allowed within
provincial powers in an attempt to make the OTA as effective as possible. After that, the dry forces had relaxed, convinced the millenni-
um had arrived and that Ontario would be dry forever. It was not
until September, a month and a half after Ferguson announced the
plebiscite, that George Nicholson of Cochrane agreed to serve as campaign chairman for the Prohibition Union.

It is difficult to imagine today the depth of feeling aroused by the liquor question. Realizing they had to deal with all the criticisms resulting from the widespread abuses of the OTA, the Prohibition Union placed large ads in daily newspapers which revealed how vicious they believed the booze trade to be. One ad stated as follows:

> Reasonable people realize that conditions produced by over a century of easy access to intoxicating liquors cannot be entirely cured in less than one-twelfth of that time. It took 20 years after legally abolishing the slavery in the U.S. to entirely eliminate the slave traffic ... There was never any thought of going back to slavery at the dictation of a minority of lawbreakers. Nor is there now in Ontario any serious thought of letting down the bars at the behest of law-evading elements that seek a system of legalized liquor sale more ruinous than the ill-famed open bar.[6]

Ads such as these appeared in newspapers across Ontario. They strummed the tunes the prohibitionists had been shouting for decades: bandit booze; the serpent that destroys our pure youth; wrecker of homes and virtue; anti-Christian; the tool of Satan; the poison that destroys the health, minds, and souls of our young men and women. In old Ontario, anti-booze sentiment ran deep. The plebiscite was held on 23 October 1924, and gave the citizen an opportunity to vote on two questions:

1. Are you in favour of the continuance of the Ontario Temperance Act?
2. Are you in favour of the sale as a beverage of beer and spirituous liquors in sealed packages under Government Control?

Election results were relayed to the public through the magic of radio. Toronto and most other large communities were thronged with crowds of expectant revellers. Early returns supported their hopes as urban voters piled up huge majorities against the OTA.

   The news brought cheers from the city crowds, who eagerly anticipated that Prohibition was coming to an end. The euphoria soon turned to concern and then dejection as the rural votes slowly reduced the wet majority. When all the returns were in, question one had been answered in the affirmative by 585,676 votes, and question two had been supported by 551,761 votes. Prohibition had won by just 33,915 votes, by far the slimmest margin of any plebiscite. In 1919, the OTA had carried by a margin of 423,508 votes.[7] Despite their lack of organization, the prohibitionists had carried the day. Since 1894, Ontario had held six plebiscites on the liquor question, and the drys had won them all.

The defeated wets were enraged, regarding the rural community as imposing its will on city folk. Ontario was threatened with a serious split. The dry majority was insisting that there should be no more plebiscites, that they had won despite the superior money and organization of the wets. It did not matter that the vote was close. The prohibitionists regarded "demon rum" as a moral issue, and they were determined to maintain Prohibition at any cost. Despite their narrow margin of victory, some prohibitionist leaders went on the offensive. On the Sunday following the plebiscite, Rev. T. Albert Moore, secretary of the Temperance Union, gave a widely reported sermon to his congregation at the Central Methodist Church on Dundas Street in London. He called on the federal government to close down the breweries and distilleries in Ontario, and end all importation into the province. Noting that Premier Ferguson had promised to vigorously enforce the OTA, he went on to state that, "we have not finished our battle yet ... the breeding places of evil must be removed."[8]

Premier Ferguson faced dissension within his party and cabinet. Many urban members feared that, at the next election, they would be turfed out by their angry constituents. In the cities there were angry outbursts against the "tyranny of the majority." In Sturgeon Falls the wets had carried the day by a margin of 1,040 to 109. The town council passed a resolution reflecting the urban frustration:

> That in view of the fact that the residents of the town of Sturgeon Falls, according to the last referendum, are not in favour of the Ontario Temperance Act and that our constables are put to extra duty to enforce the said Act, that the Chief of Police be instructed not to enforce the said law and not to do any provincial work in this connection, and that a copy of this motion be sent to the Attorney General.[9]

Many drys responded to the urban wet vote by attributing it to Jews and foreigners. A.E. Calnan, the highly respected editor of the *Picton Gazette*, which serves the rural community of Prince Edward County, dismissed the urban wet majority in an editorial headed Country vs. City. In it Calnan reasoned that the wets in clamouring for local option in the cities were being "bad losers," and that the wet majority shouldn't get special treatment because

> where did the wet majority come from? Were they composed of the votes of Canadian born citizens? Take the vote of the foreigner out of last Thursday's result and there would be a different story to tell ... an analysis of the vote in our Ontario cities would show that with the exception of those cities where there is a French vote, in practically every instance a majority of the Canadian born voters favoured ... the OTA. Are these foreigners from Central Europe to have special rights in determining the laws of our Country?[10]

In the midst of this turmoil, the premier announced that the government would exert its best efforts to enforce the Act. But Foxy Fergie had a card up his sleeve. To appease the wets he announced that scientific experiments had proven that a 4.4 percent beer was non-intoxicating and that in the legislative session of 1925, the government would introduce legislation allowing its sale in standard hotels and other outlets. Somehow Ferguson persuaded Billy Nickle, his powerful attorney general and an avowed dry, to support the legislation. It was really a temporary measure designed to stave off a revolt by the wet members of the Conservative caucus. Moderates were satisfied. Tom Moore of the Trades and Labour Council pronounced it what the working man had ordered. Many dry leaders were outraged. Former attorney general William E. Raney declared Ferguson's policy a betrayal and the "most astounding thing in the history of Canadian politics." Fortunately, the public generally was less extreme. At the *Toronto Star*, a staunch supporter of the dry cause, a sense of humour prevailed. A brewer offered a reward of $100 to any one who could get drunk on the new 4.4 beer. Reporters promptly dubbed the product "Fergie's Foam." Apparently it deserved the sobriquet as no one was ever able to claim the hundred dollars. One habitual "rubby" was widely quoted in the *Star* when, after being dragged into police court in Toronto, he described his experience with the 4.4: "That stuff? its just suds boy, just slops! Never again will I touch any of that stuff. I'm cured. You have to get drowned in it to get any effects."[11]

In preparation for the coming election, Premier Ferguson introduced legislation to redraw the electoral boundaries to redress the disproportionate number of seats allocated to the rural population.

Some rural ridings had less than a tenth of population of the more populous city ridings. Ferguson did not insist on strict representation by population, but in the redistribution, some nine dry ridings were lost and ten new urban ridings added. Hamilton received a new seat with the creation of Hamilton Centre, while new seats went to Ottawa and Windsor. Toronto, which was solidly Tory, received five new seats. Ferguson justified the increase, pointing out that even with the new seats, Toronto, with one-quarter of Ontario's population, had just one-sixth of the seats in the legislature. Former premier E.C. Drury predicted that Ferguson intended to go to the country on a government control program and trust to the "Fergymander" to get them through.[12] A little over a year later, Ferguson did just that.

Ferguson had probably decided on that course of action after the defeat of government control in the plebiscite of 1924. As the main source of opposition to his liquor policy lay in the rural ridings, it is likely he planned to call the election during the summer of 1927 when his government would have served a full four years, but more importantly, the farmers would be in their fields and many would simply be too busy to get out and vote. The poison liquor deaths which occurred across Ontario during the summer of 1926 was almost certainly the catalyst for the election call for 19 October. Ferguson undoubtedly wanted the election while the horror of the poison liquor deaths was fresh in the public mind. Certainly the Conservative Party and Ferguson himself made frequent reference to them in speeches and in campaign literature. Conservative newspaper editors mused on the tragedies effectively as, for example, in Belleville where the editor wrote:

> Even the most rabid prohibitionist admits that something is definitely wrong with the present Temperance Act. The memory of the poison liquor cases in Toronto, Hamilton, and along the Niagara frontier, is still fresh in the public mind and on a minor scale these tragedies are being repeated almost daily.[13]

In anticipation of the election, the prohibitionists had organized to support only those candidates who supported the OTA. The Toronto Conference of the (newly formed) United Church of Canada passed a resolution "to support for parliament and public life only those, irrespective of party, who will give their strength and influence to defend and maintain temperance legislation which has been endorsed by the majority of the people."[14] In practice, this meant that the Prohibition Union could support the Liberals led by W.E.N. Sinclair, or the Progressives led by William E. Raney, or Conservatives who broke with their leader's policy. This occurred in Hastings West where Billy Ireland ran as the Conservative, and H.W. Ackerman, a well-known Conservative, ran under the Prohibitionist Party banner. Of the twenty-four candidates running for the Prohibitionist Party, the best known was Nickle, the former attorney general in the Ferguson government and MPP for Kingston. Nickle had resigned his cabinet position over the government's policy. He was highly respected and his resignation threatened to provoke a split in the Conservative Party. Only the exceptional leadership skills of the premier prevented this from happening.

Despite the government's excellent record on road and highway improvement, fiscal restraint, and initiatives in developing the northern areas of the province, the election was fought almost entirely on the issue of Prohibition. Whenever Ferguson attempted to speak on something else his audience's attention would drift away, and he could only regain it by addressing the question of his government's policy on alcohol. One of his most persuasive arguments was that the revenues enriching the bootleggers would be used to reduce taxation and bring the budget into balance, a feat which had not been done for some years.

The Prohibitionist Union had powerful allies, the most notable being the *Toronto Star* which donated $5,000 to the Progressive Party and a similar sum to the Ontario Temperance Federation. Each day of the campaign, the *Star* ran the slogan, "Ferguson Government can't be trusted." Its publisher, Joseph T. Atkinson, made large personal contributions towards defeating the Conservatives. With the notable exception of the Anglicans, the Protestant churches carried out a vicious campaign against Ferguson and his policy, claiming that legal sale would result in the government becoming the supply depot for bootleggers. Each Sunday following the election announcement, Protestant ministers hammered away on the evils of drink. Frequently their sincerity and zealousness resulted in personal attacks on the premier, bordering on character assassination. Speaking at a nomination meeting in Madoc, the Reverend Stewart alleged that the "Premier was out to debauch the youth of the province."[15]

There were some notable exceptions. In Chatham, the Rev. A.C. Calder, rector of Holy Trinity Church, was elected against the Prohibitionist candidate by a comfortable margin in the riding of West Kent. In the Brantford riding, the Reverend W.G. Martin captured the seat for the Conservatives. The party also received support from such prominent clerics as the Right Reverend M.F. Fallon, bishop of the Roman Catholic diocese of London, who was widely quoted when he stated his opposition to the OTA, as "an invasion of the sphere properly belonging to morality and will support government control when I mark my ballot."[16] In Belleville, Archdeacon Beamish, rector of St. Thomas Anglican Church, who had campaigned vigorously for the Moderation League during the 1924 plebiscite, now campaigned just as strenuously for the cause of government control. He was supported in this by Father Killeen of St. Michael's parish, who spoke out against the OTA as causing a great increase in lawlessness. "I never tell my people what to do in politics," he stated, "but this is a moral issue. We must have a law that people will respect."[17] Of all the clerics to support the government, the Rev. Harry Cody of the University of Toronto – a close friend of the premier – was the most effective. In a series of radio broadcasts, he was credited with persuading thousands of "soft drys" to support the government's policy.

Unlike Ferguson, who had been able to hold together both the drys and the wets in his party, W.E.N. Sinclair, the Liberal leader, lost the support of the four French-speaking members of his caucus, all four of whom defected the party to stand as independents. A firm prohibitionist himself, Sinclair was incapable of the compromises necessary to hold together the contradictory elements of his party.

The leader of the Progressives, William E. Raney, was even less disposed to compromise. His supporters worried that his extreme attacks against the premier might cause a backlash. Raney was so convinced of the rightness of his cause, he appears to have genuinely believed that Ferguson was in the pay of the liquor interests. To disagree with Raney, was not just to be wrong but to be on the side of evil. Some of Raney's supporters were equally extreme. At Mountain View, when Sprague, who owned the canning factory, discovered that an employee, Dave Delaney, had not voted for Raney but for the Conservative candidate, he fired the man on the spot. It did not matter that Delaney was a veteran of the war and had a wife and four children to support. When the *Toronto Telegram* telephoned Sprague, he readily acknowledged that the man had been fired for voting against Prohibition and for no other reason.[18] It was the twenties' version of political correctness.

Howard Ferguson was fortunate in his opponents, but he was also a supreme tactician. Early in the campaign, he had promised the sale of beer by the glass. This was good news to the hotel keepers who were disappointed by the poor sales of the new 4.4 suds. But it caused a great uproar amongst those who saw it as return to the abuses of the open bar of pre-Prohibition days. Ferguson was approached by T.L. Kennedy, the candidate in Peel, a riding which had voted dry by a margin of four to one. "Mr. Ferguson," began Kennedy, "the man doesn't live who can win on that platform in the County of Peel. We voted eighty-six and a half per cent for Prohibition just last year and that's too great a handicap for me to overcome." Ferguson looked at Kennedy and said: "Tom, I think you're right. Now you run and don't say a word about anything. I have a card up my sleeve I haven't played yet." About three weeks later, the premier called Kennedy into his office and said, "Tom, I intend to hold a meeting in Orillia and at that meeting, I am going to withdraw beer by the glass. Now, I want you to go around to your temperance friends in Peel and tell them that you will not run unless I withdraw beer by the glass." Kennedy did as Ferguson suggested, and for decades afterwards many old timers believed he was responsible for getting Ferguson to change the party platform.[19] Tom Kennedy not only won his seat, he continued to sit in the legislature until 1959, serving briefly as premier of Ontario, and finally retiring at age eighty.

On 1 December, Ontario voters trooped to the polls in record numbers. The Tories elected 74 members, the Liberals 17, the Progressives 13, United Farmers of Ontario 3, Independents 4, and the Labour Party 1. None of the twenty-four Prohibitionist candidates were elected. Even the redoubtable Billy Nickle of Kingston was defeated. In Prince Edward County where, in the plebiscite of 1924, the drys had triumphed by 6,255 to 1,015, the Conservative candidate lost to the fiery Raney by only forty-four votes. In Hamilton Centre, one of the new ridings, former mayor Jutten easily beat his Liberal opponent. All three Hamilton seats went to the Conservatives.

For the first time in his long political career, George Halcrow, the former Independent Labour MPP, forsook his old alliances and worked to elect a Conservative candidate. He did not remain in the Conservative Party, he worked with them only on the issue of Prohibition.

West Hastings was won by Conservative candidate Billy Ireland over the dry conservative H. Ackerman. The Reverend Beamish, Archdeacon of St. Thomas Anglican Church, led the Conservative victory parade down the main street of Belleville.

The first of the new liquor stores did not open until 1 June 1927. This gave the bootleggers just six more months of easy profits, after which their illegal business began to dry up.

Under the new regime, anyone over the age of twenty-one could apply for a permit to purchase liquor. The cost of the permit was two dollars a year. Each purchase was recorded by a clerk in the Liquor Store. If a permit holder was buying unduly large amounts of liquor, he or she would be investigated. If the person was discovered to be bootlegging, they would have their permit revoked. The purchase had to be taken directly from the point of purchase to one's place of residence. A permit holder could have their permit revoked for a variety of reasons. The permit was granted on the condition of good character – a category broad enough to allow for easy cancellation.

The days of wholesale bootlegging, involving the connivance of the distilleries and breweries, was over. The Royal Commission on Customs and Excise had frightened industry executives into obeying the laws of the land. Moreover, when Premier Ferguson ended the OTA he created a legal market in Ontario for the product of these industries. They no longer had to break the law to survive.

Bootlegging in Ontario had been Rocco and Bessie Perri's principal source of income. The notoriety they received from the commission's hearings made it difficult for them to find suppliers, even for their legitimate liquor export business. Their old suppliers feared they would continue to short circuit their purchases back into Ontario. The federal cabinet now had the power to cancel the companies manufacturing licenses. Selling to Rocco and Bessie had become too risky.

In response to the changed conditions, they set up large illegal stills in Hamilton to supply their Ontario bootlegging network. They brought whisky all the way from Vancouver to supply their export business, and they used their American criminal connections to expand their narcotics trade. Ben Kerr had come out of the Commission hearings unscathed, and as a consequence, was able to continue in the liquor export business without difficulty. He continued to deliver Corby's liquor as well as beer from various Ontario and Quebec breweries. The break up of the American distilling ring in Niagara Falls had ended any incentive Perri could offer Kerr to continue as an agent of Perri's export business. Unlike Perri, Ben Kerr could still buy liquor from Ontario distilleries.

Fifteen

Courts and Commissioners

The publicity surrounding the poison liquor investigation had revealed Kerr for what he really was. No longer could he maintain the façade of the respectably successful businessman. Nevertheless, Kerr continued his theatrical portrayal of the innocent citizen, wrongly persecuted by the courts and police.

His final court appearance came on Saturday, 11 December 1926. After more than three months of postponements, Magistrate Jeffs had been advised by the special prosecutor, Peter White, that he was ready to proceed against the five defendants on the Customs Act charges. But on the morning the cases were to begin, White was not ready to proceed against Perri. After a lengthy discussion by the opposing lawyers, Kerr jumped to his feet and shouted, "All the cases can be tried here this morning. How about going on with mine. I demand that the case be heard or that the case be dismissed right now."[1] Magistrate Jeffs concurred and at 9 a.m. the case got under way. Kerr's lawyer, Col. R.H. Greer, was able to prevent the prosecution from introducing evidence on which he had not been given the required ten days prior notice. The federal government's special prosecutor was not well prepared and Greer took full advantage. The Crown was able to prove that Kerr made frequent and lengthy calls to various people in the United States, including Voelker and Webber, the bootleggers connected to the poison liquor deaths. They also introduced copies of cheques Kerr had issued to these men and to other Americans. Det. Joe Crocker had seized these cheques in Kerr's home, along with some memos to unidentified persons, giving them detailed instructions as to the use of lights along the shore. It was obvious that Kerr was using these instructions for the purpose of landing booze along a shoreline. But as long as he was landing these loads in the United States, he was not breaking the Canada Customs Act or any other Canadian law.

After some five hours of evidence and legal wrangling, the charges against Kerr were dismissed. Perri's case was not being tried that day but he remained in the courtroom and when the decision was announced, walked over to shake hands with Kerr, announcing as he did so that he was going home to eat three or four plates of spaghetti. Anyone watching this performance would have assumed that Kerr was still operating within the Perri crime family. Perhaps Perri himself believed that. Although his closest associates were Italian, the genial crime boss had been one of the first to build a criminal organization recruited from a variety of ethnic groups. His organization included men of Polish, Greek, Jewish, and Irish descent. With Prohibition in Ontario coming to an end, the export business to the U.S.A. was assuming more importance. Rocco needed to expand that part of his business to compensate for the losses to his Ontario bootlegging operation.

But Kerr had other plans. After 1926, he no longer ran loads to the western end of Lake Ontario. This was Perri's turf and Kerr stayed away from it, concentrating instead on the area between Rochester and Oswego. For reasons which can only be speculated upon, Kerr also stopped dealing with the Hatch brothers. He may have done so because the Hatch's had gone along with Bessie in 1925 and forced him to cooperate with Perri. In terms of distance, it was certainly more convenient for Kerr to deal with the Gooderham and Worts plant in Toronto rather than with Corby's, which was located north of Belleville at the eastern end of Lake Ontario.

Kerr had known Herb Hatch and Larry McGuiness since 1920, and may have felt betrayed when these long-time associates had sided with Perri. Moreover, Kerr had never stopped dealing with Corby's and got along well with their organization which included H.F. Wilkie, the plant manager, an American who replaced Billy Hume when he defected to the Hatch brothers. At the company's head office in Montreal, Harry Howlett often made the deals with the American customers. A sharp card player and bon vivant, Howlett was a shrewd judge of character who enjoyed cutting deals with the bootleggers.

Ben's customers in the United States would order a boxcar of whisky from Corby's salesman at the Montreal head office, usually paying in advance. Kerr would arrive at the Belleville docks and phone George Hudson, the office manager, or Harry Lanks, the chief cashier, advising that he was ready to pick up part of the load. Munroe, would then fill in the B-13's for Canada Customs and send the forms along with the shipper, Jim Boyle, who would go down to the docks with the workers in a Corby's truck loaded with ninety cases of whisky. Ben had organized his boat, the *Pollywog*, to maximize its carrying capacity while still leaving room for three bunks and a small galley. As long as the boat was loaded a certain way it could take ninety cases of whisky, but not one case more. Bill Lynch lived in the dock area on South Front Street and remembers how fussy and demanding Kerr was with the men loading the booze onto the *Pollywog*. "He would give the Corby's men hell if they were not careful. He wanted a felt lined conveyor so as not to hurt his boat. He would load the cases one, two, three, four – had a routine all perfected so he could get an extra two cases on board."[2]

Once the boat was loaded, Kerr would wait around the dock area, visiting with Earl McQueen and his vivacious wife, Patricia. An experienced naval man, McQueen had originally been recruited in Scotland by Herb Hatch to supervise and organize the rumrunners carrying Corby's product out of Belleville. When the Hatch brothers had left Corby's to take over Gooderham and Worts, McQueen had elected to stay on with Corby's.

Promptly at four in the afternoon, the *Pollywog* would leave Belleville, usually heading directly for its destination on the American side but sometimes stopping over at Main Duck Island. Here, Ben might visit with the lighthouse keeper, Wesley Thomas. Years later, Thomas and his wife, Illa, remember Ben as a nice, quiet man who enjoyed talking about his wife and daughter. Kerr could be very gentlemanly when the situation called for it. Although whisky was the more profitable cargo, the bulk of Kerr's business was in beer and ale. This was a simple matter of economics. The average customer in an Oswego or Rochester speakeasy could afford a lot more beer than he could liquor.

Kerr's clients would order beer by the boxcar from various breweries, including: Frontenac Brewery in Montreal, Dominion Brewery in Toronto, and Grant Springs Brewery in Hamilton. A common practice was for these breweries to ship the carload to Mid Hunt's warehouse at Deseronto. Hunt operated a warehouse in the former Rathbun buildings, located along the docks, and was licensed to store beer and ale. Rumrunners could legally pick up loads of beer at Hunt's warehouse provided it was for export to the United States. After 1926, Kerr began taking loads from the new Quinte Brewery. Located on Front Street in Belleville (just south of the Quinte Living Centre), Quinte Breweries had bought out the old Roy-Wolf Brewery. The new owner, L.W. McLennan, aggressively pursued export sales in the U.S. and quickly built up a large client base among bootleggers in northern New York state.[3] As McLennan was often on the road, Kerr usually dealt with Austin Whitten, the assistant manager and a native of Picton.

In the winter, Kerr had to change his base of operations as the ports at Belleville and Deseronto froze over. When Jack Morris Jr. began working for Kerr in the late fall of 1926, the winter base was at Whitby. A CNR spur line ran down to the Whitby docks, making transfer of the cargo to the *Pollywog* relatively easy. Young Morris had helped his father and uncle build the *Pollywog*. He had grown up around boats and had a natural talent for things mechanical. An operation for crossed eyes had left him with exceptional long distance and peripheral vision. This was useful in spotting the Coast Guard. Kerr's vision had been declining for some time, forcing him to wear eye glasses. He had initially hired young Morris after first approaching his friend, Jack Morris. The father had given his approval, regarding Kerr as a successful businessman who did not take unnecessary risks.

Kerr's decision to hire another man had arisen from his increasing concern over Alf Wheat's decline into alcoholism. By the fall of 1926, Alf's bouts with the bottle were getting out of hand. In December, his wife, Louisa, had him charged with "threatening" and he was brought before Magistrate Jeffs. Louisa testified that he became a completely different man when drinking, often forcing visiting friends and relatives out of the house. But on this last occasion, he had pointed his revolver at his wife and said "You are going to pass from this existence."[4] Magistrate Jeffs put Alf on the Indian List, which meant that he could not obtain or even drink liquor legally within the province. This restriction kept Wheat out of hotels but could not prevent him from getting booze from his bootlegging contacts. Fortunately, Louisa's action in having her husband charged brought about an improvement in Alf's drinking habits, and Kerr decided to keep him on as part of the *Pollywog*'s crew.

Jack Morris was just a teenager when he went to work for Kerr and regarded the whole thing as a great adventure. Recalling those eventful times when he was in his seventies, Morris spoke of every minute being a risk, but what he minded most was the cold. "We wore heavy woollen underwear, heavy plaid jackets, and over that a coon skin coat with a hood to cover your head. But you were always cold in winter. You wore running shoes to keep from slipping off the deck of the boat, but they didn't keep your feet warm." Morris recalls that they were chased by the Coast Guard many times but, "they could never catch us, the *Pollywog* could make about forty knots an hour and was just too fast for them."[5]

Johny Carey, a youthful rumrunner from Picton, was captured by the crew of patrol boat *131* in the waters off Oswego. Many decades later, Carey recalled that the police questioned him extensively about Kerr, a man Carey had never met or even seen. "They were awful desperate to catch him, there was a big reward for him," recalls Carey.[6] Sleek and fast, the *Pollywog* appeared to have solved Kerr's problem of the American Coast Guard. But if Kerr's concern about the Coast Guard had lessened, developments in Canada were about to impact dramatically on the business of liquor exporting.

In February of 1926, the government in Ottawa set up a Committee of the House of Commons, known as the Smuggling Committee. It was chaired by Conservative MP Harry Stevens, and its mandate was to investigate the Customs Department and the alleged wholesale smuggling of American goods into Canada which was costing Canadian retailers millions of dollars. A small businessman himself, Stevens was uncompromising in his search for corruption. As a result of the committee's work, a housecleaning of the Customs Department took place, and the minister himself, Jacques Bureau, was forced to resign and kicked upstairs to the Senate. So widespread was the corruption that even the deputy minister, R.R. Farrow, was dismissed from the service by the acting prime minister, Sir Henry Drayton.

Smugglers, who had been short circuiting loads back into Canada, were to be dealt with by a reorganized "Customs Preventative Service." A new chief was appointed and budget allocations made for automobiles and boats to more effectively patrol the Canada-U.S. border. Ontario smugglers took note of the new divisional chief, George Fowler, who was placed in charge of the force in Ontario. Stationed in Toronto, Fowler was authorized to recruit a force of fifty-five men to replace the lone officer who had previously attempted to patrol the entire province.[7] In the same year, the OPP added seventy-five new officers to its force, a number equal to the total officers on staff in 1921.

Faced with the possibility of defeat in the House over the widespread corruption revealed by Steven's Committee, the government of Prime Minister William Lyon Mackenzie King tried a classic manoeuvre. They set up a Royal Commission. Its purpose was to investigate the liquor and brewing industries with a view to determining the extent to which they had been avoiding sales and excise taxes, and to lay criminal charges where appropriate. The commission was headed up by James Thomas Brown, the chief justice of the Court of King's Bench, Saskatchewan, and by William H. Wright and Ernest Roy, justices of the Supreme Courts of Ontario and Quebec, respectively. Newton Rowell, KC, former leader of the Liberal Party in Ontario and a firm supporter of Prohibition was Commission counsel. He was assisted by R.L. Calder, KC, and two junior lawyers. They were assisted in their investigations by the RCMP, and by Major A.E. Nash, an auditor from the firm of Clarkson, Gordon, and Dilworth. The commission had the power to subpoena witnesses and compel them to testify under oath. Men like Perri and Kerr, having garnered much media attention could certainly expect to be summoned, as would the chief executive officers and top management of the breweries and distilleries.

Setting up the Royal Commission precipitated a flurry of activity. The management of O'Keefe Brewery simply destroyed their records, a few executives left the country which prevented their being compelled to testify. Some, like the Walker brothers of Detroit, sold out. Harry Hatch was able to pick up the Walker distillery business for the bargain price of $14 million.

When Perri heard that the commission was coming to Hamilton, he disappeared. Not surprisingly, the flinty Bessie Perri decided to take the stand and match wits with the commission's top lawyers. In spite of the massive evidence collected by the commissioners, Bessie initially avoided making any incriminating admissions. A few days later the Mounties managed to locate the missing Rocco and served him with a subpoena. He appeared on the stand on 4 April 1926, and proved to be as difficult to nail down as sap from a maple tree. His main line of defence was his short memory, being unable, or so it seemed, to remember anything that he had done more than a few hours previously. Nevertheless, the commission was able to prove that the Perris had lied on the stand. Bessie had claimed to have only one bank account, producing a pass book from the Canadian Bank of Commerce at King and James Streets in Hamilton, showing a balance of just $98.78. Major A.E. Nash, the auditor, managed to locate several bank accounts under various combinations such as Bessie Starkman, Bessie Perri, and Bessie Starkman Perri. These bank accounts frequently contained deposits running into hundreds of thousands of dollars. As all statements to the commission were made under oath, it was clear that Bessie Perri was guilty of perjury.

Rocco had a difficult time explaining the interview he had given to Dave Rogers of the *Star* in which he had admitted he was a bootlegger. His position was made more difficult by the fact that the *Star*'s city editor, Harry Hindmarsh, had insisted that Perri sign the newspaper proofs before running the interview. Incredibly, Rocco had

signed them. He now tried to deny that he had been able to understand what he had earlier signed. "I could not read very good English," he claimed. The testimony of various individuals and the large
number of long-distance phone calls from the Perri residence to
Gooderham and Worts, and to the Kuntz brewery, also provided sufficient circumstantial evidence to charge Rocco with perjury. In one
three-month period in 1926, over two hundred calls were made from
the Pérri mansion on Bay Street to the Gooderham and Worts distillery. No one at Gooderham and Worts or at the Kuntz brewery
admitted to doing business with the Perris. But after intense questioning, Roger Moriarity, the accountant at Grant Springs brewery,
finally admitted that his firm had sold them large quantities of beer.[8]
On 13 May 1927, Commission Chairman James Brown directed that
warrants for perjury be issued against Rocco and Bessie.

On 29 March, Kerr was called to the stand by the commission,
who tried to show that Kerr was a buyer of liquor for export and not
just a carrier. Kerr vigorously denied this but freely admitted to being
a carrier, knowing that in doing so he was not breaking any Canadian law. R.H. Calder KC conducted the questioning:

Q. Do you own boats?

A. Yes.

Q. Do you operate the boats you own?

A. Yes.

Q. For what purpose?

A. Passenger work, towing work, and liquor movements.

Q. Liquor movements?

A. Yes.

Q. What are the boats you own?

A. I do not own any now.

Q. What boats did you own?

A. The "Lark," the "Martimas," the "Voyageur," and I am contin-
ually buying, selling, repairing and disposing of them.

Q. Did you ever make any purchases from Gooderham and Worts,
Limited?

Kerr was not going to be caught so easily and replied:

"No; I do not go into that part of it at all.

Q. Did you ever transmit any orders?

A. Yes.

Q. For whom?

A. For a hundred different people.

Q. Did you ever transmit any orders for a man called Wilkes?

A. Yes.

Q. Did you ever purchase on his behalf?

A. No, on nobody's behalf.

Q. From Gooderham and Worts?

A. No. I may have delivered an envelope on his behalf on a return trip, and it may have contained money, may have contained drafts, New York drafts likely.

Q. Whatever it contained?

A. It did not make any difference to me. If they asked me to return anything like that I returned it, even if it was a roll of cash tied up with an electric band. I delivered it.

Q. And you say you never made any purchases on your own behalf?

A. They would not sell to me.

Unlike Perri, Kerr had asked for the protection of the court in order that statements he might make could not be used as evidence against him. His answers had been carefully crafted in prior consultation with his lawyer. He admitted only what the commissioners already knew. In two days of intensive questioning, the commissioners were unable to trip him up. As he appeared innocent of any wrong doing, his testimony was largely ignored by the press.

As Gooderham and Worts were now refusing to sell to the infamous Perris, Harry Hatch decided to collect on the twenty-three thousand dollars they owed the distillery. Hatch dispatched his brother Herb to the bootleggers mansion in Hamilton with orders to collect the money. The diminutive but acid-tongued Bessie flatly refused. Under pressure from Herb Hatch and Larry McGuiness, Rocco signed a promissory note for the debt. Bessie refused to sign anything, and as all the assets were in her name, it didn't matter much what Rocco signed. The decision by Harry Hatch to stop selling to the

Hamilton mobster effectively cut off Rocco's most accessible source
of supply. The Gooderham and Worts plant was not only conveniently close in Toronto, it also had its own export docks on the shore
of Lake Ontario. Henceforward, Rocco and Bessie had their liquor
shipped all the way from Vancouver. In the witch-hunt atmosphere
of the Royal Commission, none of the distilleries in Ontario wanted
to deal with them.

In 1927, Kerr and his crew were making the trip to Belleville from
Hamilton three or four times a week. From Belleville, they would
cross the lake to various drop points near Oswego or Rochester, carrying ninety cases each trip. That winter, Kerr transferred his operation to Whitby. Providing the lake was calm and ice free, the *Pollywog*
could make the crossing in two and a half to three hours. The frequency of these trips precluded Kerr from much involvement in the
Pals hockey team. He still sponsored it, but a player by the name of
Wilson took on the manager's job. The team had lost three of its top
players and was not able to duplicate the successes of the previous
year.

The *Pollywog* was one of a very few boats crossing Lake Ontario
that winter. One of its competitors was a former Russian submarine
chaser known variously as the *Uncas* or the *Butterfly*. It was sixty feet
long with a ten-foot beam, and could haul twelve hundred cases of
beer or whisky. Powered by two twelve-cylinder Liberty engines,
each of which weighed about five thousand pounds and generated
eight hundred horsepower, the *Uncas* was estimated to have a top
speed of about forty knots. Painted grey and with a low super-struc-
ture, the ship resembled a surfaced submarine. It was covered in steel
plate three-eighths of an inch thick so that normal machine gun fire
could not disable it. Rocco had purchased the *Uncas* from a rumrunning gang who had used it along the eastern Atlantic.[9] Perri's crew
operated out of Port Hope which is only fifty-five kilometres from
Whitby – Kerr's winter base. Locating the *Uncas* at Port Hope made
the interception and destruction of the *Pollywog* logistically feasible.

But Perri had more pressing problems than dealing with Kerr's
independence. On 23 April 1927, Rocco and Bessie Perri nervously
appeared in magistrate's court in Toronto where they were to stand
trial for perjury. A deal had obviously been made as the charges
against Bessie were dropped, and Rocco entered a plea of guilty to
just one of the seven counts laid against him. He was sentenced to six
months in the Ontario Reformatory in Guelph. The city was part of
his home turf, enabling him to keep in touch with Bessie and his oper-

ation. The diminutive mob boss was discharged on 27 September 1927, two months before the sentence expired.

Aside from the *Uncas* and Rocco Perri, Kerr had to be concerned with the U.S. Customs Border Patrol, which, in 1927, added two hundred more officers to patrol the shores of Lakes Erie and Ontario. Often working in conjunction with the U.S. Coast Guard, they posed a serious threat to Kerr who, if caught, faced a lengthy sentence. Moreover, the business was turning into a shooting war. In the spring of 1927, the Coast Guard reported that two rumrunners had died on Lake Ontario and two more on Lake Erie. In addition, they had wounded two smugglers while in pursuit of the *Uncas*. The Coast Guard was also increasing the frequency of its captures. In May of that year, Merle McCune, operating picket boat *2207* out of Oswego, had seized two black ships while a seventy-five-foot patrol boat had made another capture in the same waters. During the summer, the Coast Guard, often operating in conjunction with land based forces under the direction of Andrew Weidenmann, collector of customs for the port of Rochester, managed to effect at least two major seizures of rum ships a month. One of the more dramatic took place on 15 June about forty kilometres west of Oswego at Lashers Landing. Officers with the Customs Border Patrol had been keeping a close watch on Lashers Landing and were not surprised when a horse-drawn hay wagon and two automobiles came down a farmer's lane to the shore. Presently a black ship came towards them. It was commanded by "Peg Leg" Jones, a one-legged man with a reputation for ending arguments with his gun. Fortunately for the Border Patrol, Mason McCune was nearby patrolling the area in picket boat *2330*. He pulled in behind the rum ship, and when Jones tried to escape, opened fire. After a brief exchange the rumrunners surrendered. On board the *Rosella* were two hundred cases of Canadian beer. Edward "Peg Leg" Jones and his two man crew, plus the three Americans on shore, were all taken to Munroe County Jail and held on bail ranging from one thousand dollars for the smaller fry, to five thousand dollars for the infamous Jones.[10]

In the past, American law officers had made arrests of rumrunners largely as a result of tips from rival gangs or disgruntled citizens. But now the force was making frequent captures as a result of better training and equipment, and a policy of shooting to kill when necessary to prevent escape.

Jack Morris Jr. witnessed this policy first hand. The *Pollywog* was cruising towards the American shore, when it encountered a Coast

Guard picket boat. Perhaps the Coast Guard crew recognized the *Pollywog* as Kerr's boat, but whatever the reason, they opened fire on the *Pollywog* immediately. Morris got on the rear deck and piled whisky cases behind the pilot house, protecting Ben from the machine gun fire as the bullets smashed into the cases full of whisky. The *Pollywog's* superior speed enabled them to outrun the Coast Guard, but the rumrunner suffered considerable damage to its hull and pilot house. On another occasion, they were fired on at night, but most of the bullets went overhead. Morris figured the Coast Guardsman had over estimated the height of the *Pollywog's* pilot house. Even so, an examination of the boat in daylight revealed eight bullet holes. In spite of these events, the crew was confident that they had the fastest rumrunner on the lake and that nothing serious would happen to them. Looking back on his adventures with Kerr, Morris mused, "I was just lucky, a lot luckier than I realized."[11]

Sixteen

The Quebec Connection

Late in January of 1928, the Royal Commission on Customs and Excise laid its final report before the House Of Commons. The commission had previously submitted ten interim reports. They resulted in the wholesale firings of corrupt Customs officers, as well as the reorganization and strengthening of the Customs Preventative Service. The Interim Reports had also recommended that legal action be undertaken against virtually all of Canada's brewers and distillers in order to recover gallonage and sales taxes which these companies had avoided by claiming their export sales were destined for the United States when, often, their destination was to bootleggers in Canada. Legal actions were promptly begun against Gooderham and Worts, Seagrams, Walkers, and Canadian Industrial Alcohol, which owned Corby's and Wisers. The abuses of O'Keefe's Brewery and Reinhardt Brewery had been so flagrant, the government took the unprecedented step of cancelling their licenses.

On 30 December 1926, the Honourable W.D. Euler, minister of customs, announced a new policy. Henceforward, liquor exporters would have to prove they had legally landed their cargo before the government would release the double excise bond they were required to post with every export sale. In practice, this meant that rumrunners operating on the Great Lakes had to pay double the excise tax as there was no way they could legally prove their cargo had been landed in the United States. One way around this obstacle was for the liquor exporter to ship the goods to the island of St. Pierre and Miquelon. The French government would supply a landing certificate, proving the cargo had been legally exported, and the exporter could then reship the cargo on a rum ship bound for the United States. Like most European nations, the government of France regarded Prohibition as a ridiculous law and did not worry as to the eventual destination of the liquor. Consequently, after 1926, much of the liquor exported by Ontario distilleries to the U.S. went via St. Pierre and Miquelon. Some liquor was still smuggled across the lakes or the Detroit River as there was still a profit even after payment of the double excise tax. The American consul at Kingston reported to his superiors that, after 1926, about two-thirds of Corby's exports went to the island of St. Pierre and Miquelon.[1]

Beer was a different story. In Ontario, the new government liquor stores allowed a permit holder to buy only one case a month. A busy trade sprang up in illegal permits. In this way a bootlegger could assemble enough cases for a trip across the border. But the system was not practical for large scale bootleggers. Men like Kerr began bringing their beer in from Quebec. For a fee, many of Quebec's liquor store managers were willing to sell truck loads of beer to Ontario bootleggers. It was against regulations, but the Quebec Liquor Commission did not concern itself so long as the liquor left the province. Moreover, for those smugglers with orders for Scotch, champagne, or other expensive imports, the Quebec Liquor Commission's policy of importing foreign liquor for exporting outside the province conveniently by-passed the federal government's new regulation requiring that such purchases could only be made by provincial liquor commissions. As a consequence, shipments of beer to "exporters" were frequently augmented by cases of Scotch. The *Toronto Star* indignantly reported on this practice noting that

> The law, recently passed by the Canadian parliament ... makes it unlawful for anyone to ship liquor into a province unless it be consigned to the liquor control board of the province ... The foregoing appeared to strike at the business of foreign distillers, but the action of the Quebec liquor commission by permitting the exportation of liquor bought by that body ... places it in the position of a legal agent, immune to the law enacted by parliament: the product so handled is enhanced in value by reason of the added official label and wrapper of the commission ... It is placed in a warehouse and parcelled out as the demands of the smugglers warrant removal.[2]

Most of this liquor came out of Montreal. The Frontenac brewery, located in that city, became a popular source of beer for Ontario's smugglers during the latter years of Prohibition.

The federal government's attempt to clamp down on smugglers was more effective in its revitalization of the Customs Preventative Service. In the early 1920s, the force had numbered just 122 officers and men, but by 1928, the service had increased to over six hundred men. Moreover, the corrupt leaders of the Preventative Service were replaced by honest men dedicated to wiping out the smuggling traffic. The former minister of customs, Jacques Bureau, had ordered an extra bathroom installed on the HMCS *Margaret*. When it was supposedly out chasing smugglers, he was using it for private parties. When the captain of the *Margaret* actually managed to seize 806 cases of whisky, the chief of the service in Montreal ordered the booze returned to the bootleggers.[3] After the firing of the customs minister, a new captain was put in charge of the *Margaret*. Capt. Herbert Coffin was an excellent leader, capable seaman, and absolutely honest. In a short time, he racked up an impressive list of captures in the St. Lawrence River, particularly against smugglers attempting to bring liquor back into Canada from the island of St. Pierre and Miquelon.

In Ontario, the Preventative Service was increased from one man to fifty-five. They were equipped with a number of fast cars, and, initially, one motorboat which was stationed at Fort Francis. By 1928, the service had a patrol boat on Lake Ontario. In Belleville, the Preventative Service rented a slip in the boathouse of the Schuster Coal Co., located just south of the present Morton building. Kerr rented a slip for the *Pollywog* in the slip next to the Preventative Service boat. Kerr liked to joke about this, noting that the government didn't have to go far to find him.[4] Kerr knew that as long as he didn't try to run his load back into Ontario, he had nothing to fear from the Preventative Service. This was not the case with Rocco Perri. Believing that Rocco was still running booze back into Ontario, H.T. Nugent, the Preventative Service officer in Port Hope, seized Rocco's boat, the *Uncas*, on the technicality that "she had failed to report inward after delivering a cargo of liquor to the American side of Lake Ontario." Officer Nugent then wrote to the United States Treasury Department advising that the *Uncas* had been delivering ale to the American side for the past year and that this was on file with the customs office at Port Hope. In view of these facts, he suggested that, "the U.S. Coast Guard would be perfectly justified in seizing her wherever and whenever seen in American waters."[5] This was the sort of cooperation American officials had been attempting to get from Canada Customs for many years.

U.S. Coast Guard captures of rum ships on the Great Lakes peaked in 1928, averaging about one ship a week during the navigational season. More experienced crews and a greater number of patrol boats were the main reasons for this success. In fact, the Coast Guard was so successful that in succeeding years the number of captures fell off. Many of the smaller operators could not afford to stay in the business after losing one or two boats.

"Gentleman" Charlie Mills lost two boats in the summer of 1928, and after eight years of smuggling, retired broke to work on his father's farm, near Niagara Falls, New York. Capt. J. Earl McQueen, who used to joke that he was in charge of Corby's sales to Mexico, suffered several losses and finally quit in the fall of 1928, returning to Amherstburg, Ontario, to build a more permanent fortune in the marine salvage business.

Yet, even as these men quit a few new ones were getting in. Most of these lasted a very short time, quitting because of the sudden violence of the lake, or the discovery that, under fire by the Coast Guard or hijackers, they didn't have enough nerve. In the fall of 1928, Jack Copping, a well-bred youth from Rochester, told Ken McConnell, the lighthouse keeper at False Duck Island, that, "This is my last trip. I'll never do this again."[6] The lighthouse keeper was the last person to see Copping and his two friends alive. Their bodies and pieces of their boat later washed up on shore – the victims of hijackers or a capriciously violent lake.

Among the bootlegging community, Kerr had a special status. He had been smuggling booze on the lake since 1920, and was pre-eminently the King of the Lake Smugglers. Those who worked around boats and the wharf area were in awe of him. Kerr had merely to threaten something and that was enough. No one wanted to tangle with him. Even the police in Hamilton gave Kerr a wide berth. On one occasion, three U.S. Coast Guardsmen came into Hamilton spoiling for a fight. On arriving at the Bayview Hotel, they asked if Kerr was around, boasting loudly what they were going to do to him. Unfortunately for them, Kerr was present and dispatched the first man with a single punch. A few more blows were exchanged before they fled the hotel.[7]

Reflecting on Kerr's reputation, Jack Morris Jr. recalls that, "Ben knew who the hijackers were, but they wouldn't mess with him. He had that big .45 revolver which he always carried when we were runnin' booze. We kept a shotgun on the *Pollywog* and I used it to shoot ducks which we would cook and eat on the boat. If anyone tried to hijack our load, Ben knew I could handle that shotgun."

Sometime in the spring of 1928, Kerr and his crew ran into a new outfit at the port of Whitby. The Staud brothers had moved in on the bootlegging community at Rochester and were battling for control. Midge Staud, the boss of the outfit, had the backing of Samuel Bronfman and would later rent an office in Montreal, conveniently close to Seagram's head office. Midge and his brother George came to

Rochester from Cleveland and were later joined by brothers Karl and
Ed. The Stauds were all big, tough, violent men, well equipped to
drive out the competition in Rochester. Ed had been a rustler in Neva-
da but had fled to Rochester after a gun fight in which he killed a man
and had his own thumb blown off. When the "Purple Gang" tried to
move in on Rochester, the Stauds threw two gang members out a sev-
enth-storey window of the Seneca Hotel. With their western frontier
mentality, skill with six-shooters, and the backing of the Bronfmans,
the Stauds were able to drive their competition out of Rochester. The
Purple Gang returned to Detroit. Three years later the leader of the
gang, Ray Bernstein, and two gang members killed three rivals in the
infamous Collingwood murders. Bernstein and his associates
received life sentences for the killings. In a little over a year, the
Stauds' muscle had enabled them to gain control over the distribution of alcohol in Rochester. Midge Staud no longer worked on the
boat with his brother George. He had to oversee an operation involving fifteen trucks delivering beer and whisky to speakeasies throughout Rochester and the surrounding area. Occasionally, a local bootlegger would be discovered selling product not supplied by the
Stauds. The remedy was simple. A gun would be placed against the
vendor's temple and he would be persuaded to disclose the name of
his supplier. The unauthorized stock would be destroyed on the spot
and the supplier tracked down and dealt with. Independent rumrunners had their boats destroyed or were intercepted on the lake and
relieved of their cargo.

Sometime in 1928 or 1929, the Stauds acquired a new rumrunner.
Known to the Coast Guard as the *Dorthy*, but according to the Stauds'
descendants called the *Harry H*, it was fifty-four feet long and powered by three powerful, gas-guzzling engines. The Coast Guard estimated that the *Dorthy* could make fifty knots an hour (93 km/h). On
two occasions, in the summer of 1929, the Dorthy was involved in
shoot outs with the U.S. Coast Guard. Previously, the Coast Guard
had done all the shooting. Now they faced an opponent who was
heavily armoured and equipped with a .50-calibre machine gun; a
weapon more powerful than their .30-calibre Lewis guns. The Stauds
hired various men to run the *Dorthy*. According to U.S. Coast Guard
reports two of the crewmen, Jack Farrans and Gord Jenneman, had
long criminal records. A former guardsman, named McCune, captained the boat and the machine gun was operated by a one-eyed man
named Holmes. McCune was known among the bootlegging community as a particularly "tough egg."

The Canadian Preventative Service cooperated with the United States Coast Guard, deploying two men to find out where the machine guns used on the *Dorthy* were hidden. A memorandum from special undercover agent William Kelly advised his superiors in Washington that the *Dorthy* was operating out of Port Hope. Her weapons were cached aboard an unused tugboat where they were picked up by the *Dorthy* after she had left the harbour. The guns were hidden again before returning to her berth in Port Hope. The Coast Guard was never able to seize the *Dorthy* or its guns. Descendants of the Stauds claim that Midge Staud and his gang "owned the lake in the area around Rochester" – specifically from Point Breeze to Sodas Point. This was territory previously used by Ben Kerr and Butch Schenk. In 1929, Ben was still delivering to customers on the outskirts of Rochester in direct competition with the Staud brothers.

It is clear from the numerous Coast Guard memos that the *Dorthy* operated out of Port Hope. But Jack Morris Jr. remembers meeting the Stauds in Whitby. This was before they acquired the *Dorthy*. Morris was a naive teenager, but he noticed that, "Ben and Alf gave those guys a wide berth." Organized gangs were taking over bootlegging and liquor exporting, and forcing out independents like Kerr. Tough as he was, Kerr stood little or no chance against the well-organized and heavily-armed Staud gang.

Seventeen

Whisky and Ice

The presence of the Stauds may have been responsible for Ben's decision to shift his winter base from Whitby to Presqu'ile. Another reason was the presence of the Preventative Service officers stationed at Port Hope and Whitby. Taking Corby's whisky across Lake Ontario was legal in Ontario, but bringing in truck loads of beer from Quebec for export was not. Canada Customs was less likely to detect Kerr's beer smuggling operation when carried out from the relatively remote Presqu'ile Bay.

At Presqu'ile, Kerr rented a cottage from Grant Quick, who owned and operated Quick's Fishery. Presqu'ile is just a few miles south of the town of Brighton, and only forty miles from Corby's distillery. Almost deserted in winter, it was an ideal location for avoiding not only the Preventative Service but also any American gangsters looking to gun down the independent rumrunner. The outdoors man, Kerr, was in his element at Presqu'ile.

The huge profits available from the illegal booze traffic had led to the growth of organized mobs. Men like "Dutch" Schultz, Jack "Legs" Diamond, and the Chicago kinpin Al Capone had taken over the industry and squeezed out all but a few of the independents. Since breaking with Perri, Kerr had refused to deal with any of the mobs. He was reduced to supplying just two independents: Jim Corcoran of Utica and Frank Ferski of Rome, New York. Corcoran had been importing booze from Canada since the mid-twenties and possibly earlier. In its investigation into the Hamilton Brewing Association, the Royal Commission on Customs and Excise had read into evidence a letter from Corcoran ordering five hundred cases of beer, to be sent by rail, disguised as building materials. Other shipments were sent to him disguised as baled hay.[1] Corcoran was later arrested, attempting to smuggle 180 bottles of whisky into Niagara Falls, New York in a Chrysler sedan.[2]

In addition to Corby's whisky, Kerr also supplied Corcoran and Ferski with beer. This was trucked to Presqu'ile from Montreal and loaded into the cellar of the cottage. As the *Pollywog* lacked the capacity to carry a full truck load, the beer was hauled across the lake, ninety cases per trip, until the cellar was emptied.

By law, no individual could have more than one liquor permit, but Ben had a stack of them. He used these permits to purchase liquors such as brandy and champagne, which were not available from Corby's. Ferski and Corcoran would get orders for these products from their wealthier customers and Kerr would fill them by purchasing the product legally from a government liquor store. The most important man at Presqu'ile was Grant Quick. In addition to Quick's Fishery (which still operates in Brighton), Quick was the proprietor of the Presqu'ile Hotel, a summer playground for the gentry classes from Toronto and northern New York. Guy Lombardo and his Royal Canadians were a regular feature of the popular open-air Saturday night dances. The hotel closed after Thanksgiving weekend, and Kerr was able to arrange with Quick for the hotel's piano to be moved to Kerr's cottage.

Grant Quick's nephew, Purtell Quick, helped move the Baby Grand and thought it peculiar that this big, tough mariner would want a piano in his cottage. When the wind was right, the men and women working in the fishery could sometimes hear snatches of Ben's piano music mixed in with the sound of waves breaking on shore.

Purtell spent much of his life on Lake Ontario as a commercial fisherman. He recalls that the *Pollywog* was the only rumrunner that ever ran out of Presqu'ile Bay in winter time. "I thought he was crazy to do it," says Quick. "Sometimes there were fields of pack ice as large as three or four hundred acres." Ben would have to skirt these or, if he got caught, use his props and bow to beat the *Pollywog* out of the ice.

Ben and Alf generally avoided contact with the locals. Kerr knew that the American Coast Guard hired informers to find out when the smugglers left with their cargo. When Don Vincent, a local farmer, tried to take a photo of the *Pollywog*, Ben snatched the camera out of the man's hands and smashed it against the shore wall. Vincent, a big man, told the story many times, claiming that Kerr had booted him in the rear and that he had been so frightened he ran all the way to Brighton – a distance of three miles.

One of the few locals Ben and Alf had much contact with was Gerald Wright, who worked for his father at Wright's Garage on the main street of Brighton. Kerr had Wright's Garage do all the mechanical work on his Willys Knight sedan. A skilled mechanic himself, Kerr knew that the Wrights employed a particularly good mechanic and insisted that no other person be allowed to work on his car.

Many years later, Wright recalled one memorable encounter with Ben Kerr. "The phone rang at the garage about 6 p.m. It was snowing and blowing outside so that you could hardly see across the street. It was our smuggler [Kerr]. He was stuck and insisted that we come and get him. We took off up the Main Street to the first corner, missed it by a few feet and nearly turned the crane over. We got straightened out and headed south for about three miles. My brother and a friend stood on a fender hollering which way to turn – left or right. We moved along at about ten miles per hour until we went off the end of the road into the ditch ... we were able to back out and turn west. We found him [Kerr] about a half mile further on. It was snowing so hard by then, the inside of his car was covered with snow, but he insisted we take him back to his boat - an additional four miles. He said he knew the road and would walk ahead so as to guide us if necessary.

"Actually, there wasn't that much choice," recalls Wright. "We were three teenagers and he was a huge, raw-boned six-footer and all muscle, to boot. So we started on. He was as good as his word. He walked ahead and we followed. When we got there, we saw that his boat was frozen in, but not enough to damage it." In appreciation for their help, Ben showed the three young men around his powerful speedboat, and then took them to his cottage to warm them up. Wright recalls, "he had every kind of liquor that was ever distilled in there, but just then we were more interested in getting back ... I think it was the longest twelve-mile trip I ever drove."[3]

Jack Morris had quit working for Ben Kerr in the fall of 1928, shortly before Kerr and Wheat moved into the cottage at Presqu'ile Bay. Morris believed that Ben was taking too many risks. Speaking about his experiences years later, Morris recalled that Kerr was just too confident in his abilities. On one trip, the *Pollywog* used up much of its emergency gasoline supply, skirting large fields of pack ice which had drifted out into the lake. "We made it back to Hamilton," recalled Morris, "with no more than a gallon of gas left in the tanks." When Jack brought up the matter, Kerr replied, "Hell, I've been on this lake for years. I know what I'm doing." Jack Morris was raised in a family of boat builders and had a healthy respect for the dangers of travelling on the lake in winter. He had survived numerous brushes with the American Coast Guard, including two instances in which the *Pollywog* had been shot up, but he was not prepared to spend another winter travelling the lake with Kerr.

Both Kerr and Wheat had their reasons for continuing to cross the lake that winter. Kerr decided to carry on for one more season in order to raise money to expand his marine operation in Hamilton. Alf Wheat's wife, Louisa, had given birth to a son the previous April. He and Louisa had a large family and needed the extra money in order to buy the house they rented in Hamilton.

The two middle-aged mariners survived a close call in late January when the *Pollywog* became trapped in ice on the return leg of a trip to Rochester. The two men spent a frigid night less than five miles from shore. During the next day, the wind shifted, breaking up the ice, allowing the two half-frozen men to get back to Presqu'ile. Kerr told Purtell Quick about their close call. Perhaps the experience reinforced Ben's view that he was invincible: he had faced the worst the lake had to offer and survived.

On Sunday, 24 February 1929, Kerr and Wheat prepared to take a load of beer across the lake. Wheat phoned home and spoke to his wife, Louisa, and then asked to speak to each of the children. Fred Wilkinson, Alf's stepson, was out skating on the harbour, and Alf told Louisa to be sure and tell young Fred that he had his birthday present, and would be bringing it home soon.

The *Pollywog* and her crew did not return the next day as expected. Purtell Quick decided to drive down to the bluff (Proctor's Point) where he could look out over the bay. He thought the *Pollywog* might be trapped in offshore ice. It had been a mild winter with a great deal of snow; drifts as high as six feet prevented Quick's Model-T Ford from reaching Proctor's Point, and Quick had to turn back. Kerr had said he might go directly to Hamilton after delivering the booze, and Purtell concluded that must be what he had done.

It took almost a week for their families and business associates to realize that the men were missing. Six days after their disappearance, the two American bootleggers Frank Ferski and James Corcoran charted a seaplane at Syracuse and flew out to Main Duck Island. But heavy fog impeded their search and they could not determine if the men had made it to the island. The following day, Jack Beebe, who claimed to be Kerr's brother-in-law, and Allan Crowley, a friend from Hamilton, chartered a plane at the Kingston Flying Club and flew along the lake from Kingston to Brighton, again without results. However, a report came in that someone had spotted what appeared to be an overturned boat south of Main Duck Island. That night, Louisa May Kerr phoned an official at Corby's. She had heard the report of the overturned boat and was concerned that Ben and Alf had drowned. The Corby's official assured Louisa that if her husband and Wheat had reached Main Duck they would be safe. Claude "King" Cole, who owned the island, kept two men on the island over the winter to take care of his livestock. Unfortunately, there was no phone at Main Duck and therefore no way to communicate with the caretakers.

On Tuesday, Walter Leavens, of Leavens Brothers Air Service, was hired by Jack Beebe to search the eastern end of the lake. Beebe was Kerr's assistant, helping out with the running of the marina in Hamilton and doing whatever odd jobs Ben needed done. The Leavens Brothers were barnstormers in the Canadian bush pilot tradition. They operated their outfit from the family farm at the eastern end of Belleville, (on Hwy. 2, where Baz Auto is today), but in winter flew off the Bay of Quinte from the bottom of Foster Avenue. Walt Leavens took Jack Beebe up in an "Eagle Rock," an open cockpit biplane with a cruising speed of seventy knots (130 km/h). The two men made a circuit of Prince Edward County, frequently dipping the aircraft's wings to improve their view of the shoreline below. They then flew out to Main Duck Island to check out the sighting of an overturned boat. No trace of boat or men was found and the searchers concluded that the boat sighting was just a hump of black ice which had formed on a shoal or bar off Main Duck. Mountainous blocks of ice were piled high around the island, making any landing or approach by boat impossible.

In the meantime, lights were spotted flashing at night from Main Duck, leading Beebe and the searchers to conclude that the two rumrunners had some how made it to the island. It was assumed that the island's caretaker, Alex Taylor, was using the Lighthouse light to signal that the men were safe. As they could do nothing further until the ice cleared and allowed travel to Main Duck, Jack Beebe and friend Allan Crowley returned to Hamilton while Frank Ferski and Jim Corcoran returned to the States.

Now calling himself "Colonel Beebe," Jack Beebe showed up the next week in Picton, driving Kerr's Willys Knight sedan and towing a boat and motor. Along the way, he had picked up Bill Young from Brighton. On the weekend, they moved out to Point Traverse, staying in a cottage owned by Henry Bongard, where they waited for an opportunity to cross the twenty kilometres of lake to Main Duck Island. A steady western wind had blown pack ice into the entire eastern end of the lake, forcing the two men to wait for the wind to shift and move the ice back out.

Beebe, whose vivid imagination had him assuming the title of colonel one week and Ben's brother-in-law the next, no doubt regaled his captive audience of one with stories of his derring-do on the lake and in the military. With Beebe it was always difficult to separate fiction from fact.

Rumours began to circulate that the *Pollywog* and its crew had been hijacked. Either Corcoran or Ferski let it be known that Kerr was carrying several thousand dollars when they last saw him on the evening of the 24 February. Police and newsmen recalled the fifty-foot rumrunner *Seahawk* which had been found the year before in Pleasant Bay, frozen in thirty feet of ice. Two of its four crew members floated to the surface in the spring, but the others were never found, and the cruiser had been stripped of everything of value. Its captain was reported to be carrying $5,000, leading many to believe that a gang of hijackers was operating out of Prince Edward County. Rumours of a possible hijacking drifted back to Louisa Wheat and Louisa Kerr, both of whom were now sick with worry.

The men had been missing for three weeks and Louisa May was growing desperate. Perhaps not satisfied that Jack Beebe was sufficiently competent, she phoned Jack Morris Jr., asking him if he would help. "You know all the places they go Jack," she had implored. Jack could not refuse the request. He had always had the highest respect for Mrs. Kerr, whom he described as a "very attractive woman and a real lady." Morris showed up in Picton on Wednesday, 21 March, and assured reporters from the *Picton Gazette*, *Daily Ontario*, and *Kingston Whig Standard* that the men would be found safely at Main Duck Island. Morris, who was just twenty years of age, told the reporters, "When I was with Kerr, we always made for the Ducks in case of trouble."[4] Further hope arose from reports that the light from Main Duck had been seen for the past three nights.

These hopes were quickly dashed. On Wednesday, 22 March, Jack Beebe and Bill Young were finally able to get through the ice to Main Duck. The caretakers reported to Beebe they had seen no one, and that the light had not been shining from Main Duck, but from Galloo Island, further to the south, where an outbreak of rabies was decimating the animals at the fox farm. A search of the shoreline turned up nothing, and Beebe was forced to conclude that Kerr and Wheat were not there. The *Kingston Whig Standard* ran the story under the headline, "No Hope Remains for Missing Men."[5]

Aaron McGlennon was living at his parents' farm east of Colborne – about a hundred kilometres north-northwest of Main Duck

Island – when he heard about the missing men. Someone at the local hotel told him that the U.S. Coast Guard was offering a $5,000 reward for Kerr. To the twenty-four-year-old farmer this was a fortune. It was enough money to buy his own farm and to equip it with livestock and machinery. Ever since he could remember, Aaron and his brother had walked along the shoreline of Lake Ontario in the spring after the ice had gone out. "We often found things we could use. There was more shipping in those days and often times we would find parts of boats and other things washed ashore."[6]

On a cool Wednesday afternoon, Aaron was walking along the shore with his collie Bluff, when the dog started barking at something under the roots of a tree. Aaron went over and was startled when he recognized that Bluff had found the hand of a man and some human bones. After the initial shock, he returned home and phoned the OPP. The bones were placed in the McGlennon's empty chicken coop. Officer McBrien came out and removed the bones – but not before Aaron's mother had gone out to the coop and received quite a shock. No one had told her the bones were there.

Wheat's son Len came down and was able to identify the remains as those of his father from the name "Rose" tattooed on the hand – the name of Alf's first wife. Four policemen came down from Hamilton to investigate the death, while Len made preparations to take his father's body back on the train. The Brighton coroner, Doctor Dure, ordered an inquest which was held the next day and then adjourned for a week.

In the meantime, Aaron continued to patrol the shoreline in front of the farm. Early on Saturday morning he and Bluff found the body of Ben Kerr. It was floating just offshore. Unlike Wheat, Kerr's body was largely intact, although somewhat swollen from its time in the water. With the exception of one woollen sock, the action of the ice had worn off all Ben's clothes and the face was not recognizable. The sock, knitted by Ben's mother, provided definite identification of the remains.

Aaron McGlennon is an elderly man now, but he still has a clear memory of that morning. "It was an awful shock," he says, "I had nightmares over it for a long time." Later, McGlennon and his neighbours would find parts of the *Pollywog*, including two fifty-gallon gas tanks and one one-hundred-gallon tank. They were all empty. Sometime in April wreckage from the *Pollywog* was washed ashore. Grant Quick came down and identified the keel and one of the propellers. He later used the prop for various boats belonging to the Quick Fishery.

On Saturday evening, 30 March, twenty-year-old Leonard Wheat boarded the train at Brighton on his father's last trip home. With him were the four policemen. The bodies of Kerr and Wheat were in a locked car in the back of the train. Whether the men had died by natural causes or by persons unknown had not yet been determined. But Len Wheat remained convinced for the rest of his life that his father and Ben Kerr had been murdered by gangsters or hijackers. Other players in the drama had different opinions.

Eighteen

Murder or Misadventure?

What really happened to Kerr and Wheat?

The daughter of Kerr believes her father was murdered, probably by hijackers or rivals. This is also the view held by some of the descendants of Alf Wheat, including stepson, Fred Wilkinson, and Len Wheat, the young man who claimed the bodies.

The most likely suspects would be Perri or the Staud brothers. The methods used by the Staud brothers to deal with the Purple Gang shows that they were capable of murder. But they lacked the means to carry out the job. Coast Guard reports reveal that they did not acquire the *Dorthy* (or *Harry H*) until the summer of 1929. Midge Staud's eldest son remembers that his father started rumrunning in 1928, using a converted twenty-eight-foot pleasure boat which was not equipped to run in the winter. In the winter of 1928-29, the Stauds were not yet in control of the Rochester territory. They had yet to deal with the Purple Gang who were a much greater threat to their operation in that city than was Ben Kerr. In addition, they did not acquire the means to take on Ben and the *Pollywog* until the spring of 1929 when they purchased the *Dorthy*. This leaves Rocco and Bessie Perri as the most likely suspects.

Outwardly genial and charming, Rocco was a ruthless gangster, greatly feared within the Italian community of Hamilton and the Niagara peninsula. As RCMP Corporal Webster reported in an undercover operation, "There is not an Italian in Hamilton who will give this man away ... Perry [sic] is a clever and dangerous crook exercising an extraordinary influence over the men in his employ, and any who are not in his employ are afraid of him. He is the 'King-pin' directing all operations, but the members of his gang when caught shoulder the responsibility and pay the penalty."

Rocco and Bessie certainly had the means to intercept and destroy the *Pollywog*. The *Uncas*, was faster and much better armoured than Kerr's boat. On 30-31 of October 1929, the crew of Coast Guard patrol boat *9001* captured the *Uncas* off Point Abino on Lake Erie, wounding two of its three crewmen in the process. Surprisingly, the *Uncas* did not carry any machine guns or other

weapons. This was consistent with Perri's statement to the *Star* some
years earlier that his men did not carry guns. The *Uncas* was found to
be registered to Amos "Nick" Vandeveer of Port Colborne, an infamous and daring smuggler connected to the Perri organization. Vandeveer was an experienced seaman who often operated his boats
himself. He was certainly capable of intercepting the *Pollywog* on
Lake Ontario but was not experienced at winter boating. Lake Erie
freezes over in winter and Vandeveer was not known to have operated on Lake Ontario, confining his operations to Port Colborne and
Lake Erie. Nor was he ever known to be involved in any criminal
activity other than rumrunning.

After Prohibition, Vandeveer moved to northern Ontario where
he operated a sawmill until his retirement. While it is unlikely that
Vandeveer would have gone after the *Pollywog*, that did not preclude
Perri from hiring someone else to do the job. Rocco may also have had
a motive.

The court scene where Kerr was acquitted would indicate that the
two men had parted on good terms. Moreover, Kerr was operating at
the eastern end of Lake Ontario, well away from Perri's territory. Jack
Morris also confirmed that Kerr was no longer smuggling booze or
alcohol back into Canada but confining his operation to taking liquor
into the United States. Perri's only motive lay in the possibility that
Kerr knew too much about the poison liquor deaths. If Kerr was captured by the Americans, he might trade information to avoid a long
sentence. The possibility that Kerr had that kind of information is
doubtful, as Perri was always careful to use others to insulate himself
from the actual crimes. Unlike Kerr, who participated actively in the
business of smuggling, Perri always ordered things done by others.
Perri had the means to have Kerr and Wheat murdered, and he may
have had the motive, but the evidence must be found elsewhere.

Unfortunately, the official report of the inquest has not survived,
but the *Daily Ontario* of 19 April 1929, gives a detailed account of the
findings. Doctor Dure and Crown Attorney W.F. Kerr, KC, concluded "that death was accidental, there having been no evidence of foul
play." The newspaper account noted that Kerr's head had been
crushed off. Perhaps he could have been shot in the head without the
medical examination detecting any trauma to the body. But Aaron
McGlennon, who was present at the autopsy, remembers quite clearly that Kerr's head was not crushed off, but rather flattened from the
effect of the water and ice. McGlennon's recollection precludes the
possibility that Kerr was shot. The body, he remembers, was in sur-

prisingly good condition, the result of having being immersed in extremely cold water. In his opinion, the men had died from exposure to the cold water. He agrees with the findings of Doctor Dore and the Crown attorney.

Purtell Quick, who was the last person to see the two men alive on this side of Lake Ontario, agrees with McGlennon and adds some information which further strengthens this conclusion. During the search for the men, Quick spoke with the Americans to whom Kerr had delivered his cargo that night. They told him that the *Pollywog* had damaged one of its propellers beating its way through the floating ice fields while crossing to the American side. The ice fields were extensive, some covering three to four hundred acres. The *Pollywog* had used up a great deal of reserve gasoline getting through them. They had urged him to get additional gasoline supplies, which were available on shore, but Kerr was intensely afraid of rotting away in an American jail. He didn't want to go ashore for gas and take a chance on being captured by the Border Patrol. He told Jim Corcoran that he thought he had enough gasoline to make it back.

Jack Morris Jr. held the same view as Purtell Quick. He quit travelling with Kerr in the fall of 1928 because he felt that Kerr was always cutting it too close by not allowing enough reserve gas for emergencies. Aaron McGlennon found two of the gas tanks from the *Pollywog* and spoke to Harry Hubble who found the other one. "There was no gas in any of them," recalls McGlennon.

The final evidence as to the fate of the *Pollywog* and its occupants did not turn up until the summer of 1994. Two sports fisherman from Colborne, Tim Rawn and Tom Nelson, were crossing the waters in front of McGlennon's Point. Heavy fog forced them to reduce their boat's speed so that it was barely making steerage. Nelson spotted something glinting off the bottom of the lake. The two men decided to investigate. Donning flippers and masks, they explored the area, finding two marine engines, various mechanical parts, and two marine carburetors. The water in that area is only about ten feet deep. It was the shiny brass carburetors that attracted their attention. The author went out with these men and discovered that the *Pollywog*'s remains lie no more than a hundred yards from shore – just at the normal limits of shore ice in winter. One of the Kermath engines is wedged behind a large boulder, indicating that the *Pollywog* sunk on or near that spot. The other engine is not wedged and lies some distance away. No doubt, the waves and ice have moved it further out into the lake over the past sixty-five years.

One thing that puzzles is the fact that there is still gasoline in one of the carburetors. The most probable explanation is that Kerr realized he did not have enough gas to get the *Pollywog* into Presqu'ile and decided to let the wind, which was coming out of the southeast, blow the boat in close to shore where he would use his remaining gas supply to make a landing. If the shore ice was too thick for a man to climb, Kerr could power the *Pollywog* to a place where the ice was less thick.

Aaron McGlennon spent seventy-odd years on the family farm which fronts on Lake Ontario. "At that time of year," he says, "the shore ice along our property is too steep for a man to climb." Kerr was so close to shore, he may have felt the water would be shallow enough for he and Alf to wade in. But it was not. Had the *Pollywog* been able to get another fifty feet towards shore, the two smugglers would probably have made it.

A neighbour of Aaron McGlennon's testified at the inquest that she saw lights flashing out on the lake the night the two men disappeared. Realizing he was down to his last few ounces of gas, Kerr was likely flashing his lights to attract assistance.

At some point the storm forced the *Pollywog* into the ice. The wreckage indicates the hull split in the middle, sending the two men into the icy waters where they would have been overcome by hypothermia in a few minutes. After sixty-five years, the finding of the wreck by Rawn and Nelson ends all speculation.

Ben Kerr and Alf Wheat died in the lake, victims of Kerr's overconfidence in his mariner's ability, and his fear of capture by the Americans. Unfortunately for Alf Wheat, the King of the Rumrunners had used up his luck. Wheat left a widow with four children still at home; the youngest, Eric, was just ten months old at the time of his father's disappearance.

Epilogue

Late in the evening of 13 August 1930, Rocco and Bessie Perri returned home from a visit with friends and drove their car into the garage at the rear of their home on Bay Street. Two men emerged from the blackness of the garage and shotgunned Bessie. Apparently, she was the hitmen's only target. She died almost instantly.

Emulating the Chicago gangsters, Rocco staged a funeral in the grand style, buying his "late and lamented" an ornate bronze coffin trimmed in silver. The hearse was followed by fifteen open vehicles, each one carrying elaborate and expensive floral arrangements. Rocco extended an open invitation to the public to attend the funeral. So many turned up that it threatened to turn into a mob scene. Pickpockets, circulating amongst the curious, were reported to have cleaned up. Bessie's murder has remained a mystery to this day, but the available evidence indicates that she was shot by mobsters from Rochester for welching on a drug debt.

Without his shrewd *amoretto*, Perri's fortunes declined steadily. In 1933, he was forced to spend ten days in jail for failing to pay a twenty dollar car repair bill. He made a partial comeback, but never again achieved his old status as King of the Bootleggers. In 1940, the government found a way to take him out of circulation altogether. As Italy was fighting on the side of Nazi Germany, the government was able to inter Perri at Camp Petawawa as an enemy alien. Italy switched to the Allied side in 1943, and Rocco was released that October.

On the surface, Perri appeared to have gone straight, taking a job as a janitor at the Metro theatre at the corner of Bloor and Ossington Streets in Toronto. In fact, the theatre was owned by his latest partner in love and crime, Annie Newman. Rocco and Annie were laying plans to regain control of his old territory. The Buffalo-based Magaddino crime family controlled most of the mob in southern Ontario and knew of Perri's plans. On one of his frequent trips to Hamilton, he visited his cousin, Joe Serge, examined his property at 166 Bay Street South, and made arrangements with his lawyer to have the tenants evicted. He was either preparing to sell the house or move back and use it as a base of operations. The next day, Sunday, 23 April 1944, Rocco, complaining of a headache, left his cousin's house to go for a walk. He left his locked sedan on the street nearby. Rocco Perri was never seen again. Both the police and the criminal elements in Hamilton believe that Rocco was "taken for a ride," and his body dumped in a barrel filled with cement. It is widely believed that the body of Canada's "little Caesar" now rests at the bottom of Hamilton Bay.

Jack Morris Jr. took over Morris Boat Works from his father and uncle and continued the family boat building tradition for many years. The advent of fibreglass boats gradually eliminated the wooden boat builders until Morris was the only one still plying the trade in the Hamilton area. That era ended in 1972 when Jack Morris ended three generations of tradition by closing the Morris Boat Works.

In the summer of 1951, a fire did fifty thousand dollars damage to Kerr's boathouses, destroying one whole section of the storage units. By the early 1970s, the boat houses were in such a state of collapse they had to be torn down. A modern marina now occupies the site.

Louisa May Kerr continued to live in the house on Bay Street North which her husband had built with his rumrunning profits. She and her daughter, Helen, lived in comfort on the money Ben had accumulated, and on the revenue from the rental of the boat storage units. Helen set up a dancing school which she operated from the house for several years. In 1944, she married Flight Lieutenant John Binks. Later, they started up Hamilton Medical Laboratories. Helen and her husband continued to live with her mother in the house on Bay Street.

Binks died suddenly of a heart attack in 1961. Helen did not remarry but continued to live with her aging mother in the big house on Bay Street North. They were both active in Christ's Church Cathedral. Helen was employed at CHCH television station and was active in various theatrical organizations. Both women continued to live in the house until their respective deaths. Louisa Kerr died in January of 1979, almost fifty years after the disappearance of her husband on Lake Ontario. Her obituary in the *Hamilton Spectator* makes no mention of Ben Kerr but described her as, "the beloved wife of the late Charles J. Kerr, (the name of Ben's father), loved mother of Mrs. Helen Binks." Five years later, Helen died of cancer. She had time to arrange her affairs, including the disposal of the house built six decades earlier from her father's rumrunning profits. The family lawyer was instructed on the obituary which described Helen as the daughter of

"Charles J. Kerr." Both mother and daughter effectively denied Ben Kerr's existence.

But the daring smuggler was too bold and colourful a character to disappear so easily. At Presqu'ile, now a provincial park famous for its birds and monarch butterflies, a new marine museum is being erected. Its architects are recreating some of the colourful characters who frequented Presqu'ile. One of these is the eighteenth-century pirate, Bill Johnson. The other is Ben Kerr.

Using modern technology, a "ghost" of Kerr will appear before visitors in the museum and speak to them about his days as a smuggler. The damaged prop from the *Pollywog*, found by the two fishermen in the summer of 1994, will also be on display. Fittingly, the ghost of Ben Kerr, dormant for seventy years, is returning to the scene of his death. Old smugglers, it seems, do not fade away.

Eight years ago Hamilton May, the present owner of the old McGlennon farm, erected a large wooden cross on his property. May had heard of the drowning of the two men but his action was personal and had nothing to do with Ben Kerr or the *Pollywog*. In fact, Hamilton May had no idea that the remains of the *Pollywog* lay so close to his property. The cross is about ten feet high and stands sentinel on a lonely bluff directly overlooking the wreck of the *Pollywog*. Years ago, May attached a metal plate to the centre of the cross. The plate reads:

Jesus calls over life's restless sea
Christians, follow me.

The irreverent old smuggler would have gotten a chuckle over that.

Notes

One: Double Death

The material for this chapter is derived primarily from interviews with Helen (Kerr) Binks, Jack Morris Jr., Len Wheat, Elizabeth Wheat, Sandra (Morris) Stokes, the records of Blatchford and Wray Funeral Home (on microfilm at the Hamilton Public Library), and articles in the *Hamilton Spectator* dealing with the funeral, 2 April 1929, as well as the *Daily Ontario*, 30 March 1929. The violent storm is extensively described in the newspapers of the day.

Two: The Strike and the Piano Player

The Hamilton streetcar strike is extensively covered in the Hamilton *Spectator* and the Hamilton *Herald*.. Kerr's role in the strike was described by his nephew John Ben Kerr. Kerr's manner of dressing was obtained from the newspaper and from interviews with Kelly Thompson, Dan `Mickey' Ward who worked for Ben in his marina, and from Ray Murphy, who lived on the same street as the Kerrs, and who in the tenth decade of his life has a remarkable memory. The Adam Clark Company, now based in Burlington, has timesheets and pay records of the period.

Three: The Riot Act

The material for this chapter is found primarily in the Hamilton *Spectator* for the months of November and December, 1906. The events are later recalled in the issues of 4 February 1960, 16 November 1963, and 19 August 1982. John Benjamin Kerr, nephew of Ben Kerr, confirmed the family story concerning Ben's attacking the soldiers with the piano stool.

1. *Hamilton Spectator*, 4 February 1960.

2. Ibid.

3. Ibid, 6 December 1906.

4. Ibid, 4 February 1960.

5. Ibid.

6. Ibid, 17 December 1906.

7. *Hamilton Herald*, 13 December 1906, editorial page.

Four: Power Boats and Politics

1. *Hamilton Times*, 1 March 1905.

2. Ibid.

3. The Magazine of Industry 1910, *The Daily Times*, Hamilton Ontario, 1910, p. 79.

4. Wentworth County Registry Office, instrument 214397, Lot 7, Plan 127.

5. *Hamilton Daily Times*, 1 April 1912.

6. The wedding and honey-moon trip is described in the *Hamilton Spectator*, 14 September 1912. The author has some of Mrs. Kerr's calling cards.

7. The marriage of George Kerr and Helen Bews is described in the *Hamilton Spectator*, 21 June 1906.

8. The strike is described in The *Hamilton Herald*, 1 May 1907. The positions held by the men in Local 67 is in ,*Organized for Action, 90th Anniversary, 1899-1989.* a booklet published by Local 67 of the United Association of Journeymen and Apprentices of the Plumbing and Pipe Fitting Industry, *Hamilton*, 1989, p. 18 and Appendices D and E.

9. *Hamilton Herald*, 14 February 1914.

10. *Hamilton Herald*, 10 February 1916, and 20 May 1916.

11. *Hamilton Spectator*, 21 September 1916, and *Herald* Scrapbooks, Vol. El.1, Elections Municipal, p. 70, Hamilton Public Library.

12. "Hamilton's Grand Old Man of Politics Lives With Memories," *Hamilton Spectator*, 9 February 1961.

Five: Prohibition Comes to Ontario

1. Interview with Maxwell Henderson, former auditor general of Canada, 16 May 1985.

2. *Toronto Daily Star*, 10 June 1915.

3. Nicholson, Colonel G.W.L. *Official History of the Canadian Army in the First World War, Canadian Expeditionary Force 1914-1919.* Queen's Printer, Ottawa, 1964, pp. 546 and 548.

4. *Toronto Daily Star*, 26 November 1915.

5. *Toronto Daily Star*, 14 September 1916.

6. *Daily Intelligencer*, 10 June 1922.

7. *Hamilton Spectator*, 15 October 1919.

Six: Piano Player to Rumrunner

1. *Hamilton Spectator*, 4 October 1919.

2. Kelly Thompson, son of Jim Thompson, remembers Kerr being there a lot. Mickey Ward, who worked for Kerr part-time, saw both men there and thought they were friends.

3. In the old Kerr home is a printed cardboard sign bearing that message.

4. Interview with Wes Thomas, South Bay, 5 November 1982.

5. Some of the records of the Morris Boat Works have survived and are in the possession of the daughter of Jack Morris Jr., Mrs. Sandra Stokes. These records reveal that as far back as 1916 Morris was doing repairs to the twenty-eight foot cruiser, and that in 1919, Morris built a thirty-two foot runabout for Kerr.

6. *Daily Intelligencer*, 6 June 1922.

7. Rochester *Democrat*, 18 January 1920.

8. Patrick O'Learly, a partner in the National Import Co. of Mexico City, testified in the trial of George Woodward that he deposited $20,000 or more with Hatch in Montreal as part of setting up delivery with Corby's. Belleville *Intelligencer*, 16 May 1922.

Seven: "In the Event of My Death ..."

1. Interview, Don Harrison, Trenton, September 3, 1984.

2. Welbanks confirmed Harrison's story.

3. A copy of the will is in the Wentworth County Registry office.

4. Interviews: Wes Thomas, Wellington, 5 November 1982, and Jack Morris Jr., Hamilton, 3 December 1983.

5. Don Harrison, ibid.

6. Appas Tappas in the *Globe and Mail*, 15 May 1941. *Martimas* won the race in 1898. George M. Hendrie, the owner, donated part of the winnings to the Hamilton General Hospital. A section of the Hospital was subsequently named the Martimas Wing.

7. Thomas M. Coffee, *The Long Thirst*. W.W. Norton and Co., New York, 1975, p. 111.

8. *Hamilton Herald*, 30 October, 3 November, and 5 November, 1919.

9. *Hamilton Spectator*, 9 February 1961.

10. *Telegram*, 18 April 1921.

Eight: The Crime Boss and the Independent

1. This information was discovered by James Dubro and Robin Rowland, (after the publication of their book on Rocco Perri), in the PAO, Arson file - 1912, RG 23 E 38, Box 1. They made the information available for this book.

2. Dubro, James, and Rowland, Robin F. *King of the Mob*. Penguin Books Canada, Markham, 1987, p. 37.

3. *Financial Post*, 15 October 1926.

4. *Toronto Daily Star*, 19 November 1924.

5. PAC, National Personnel Records, citation and information on awarding of medals to A. Wheat.

6. Interview, Fred Wilkinson, Simcoe, 8 January 1994.

7. PAO, letter to Colonel Price, acting Attorney General, R.G. 23, E 93, 1.9 File 1. The report is undated but is likely from 1925, following the Perri's sensational interview with the *Star* in November of 1924.

8. HPL, *Herald* Scrapbooks, Vol. H-1, Harbour, p. 85.

9. Interview, Kelly Thompson, Hamilton, 29 September 1993.

Nine: Turning the Tide against the Law Breakers

1. AO, Annual Report OPP, 1924.

2. *Toronto Star*, 20 November 1923.

3. *Daily Intelligencer*, 9 October 1919.

4. Ernest H. Charrington, *Anti-Saloon League Year Book 1925*, New York, Anti-Saloon League of America, p. 11.

5. USNA, Coast Guard, report dated 12 January 1925.

6. *Hamilton Spectator*, 9 January 1925.

Ten: John Brown Goes to Jail

1. Don Harrison, op. cit.

2. Ben is quoted by the Rochester *Democrat and Chronicle*, 27 May 1925.

3. Ibid, 26 May 1925, 30 May 1925, 1 June 1925.

4. Ibid, 1 June 1925.

5. Ibid, 30 May 1925.

6. *Brockport Post*, 13 February 1990.

7. Ibid, 23 July 1990.

8. USNA, Department of State, File No. 811.4

9. *Rochester Democrat-Chronicle*, 27 May 1925.

10. Ibid, 29 May 1925.

11. The author pursued the papers for two months after the trial with no further mention of Mae Davis. The USNA has no record of her being charged with any other crime.

12. *Rochester Democrat and Chronicle*, 16 June 1925.

Eleven: Five Thousand Dollars for Charity

1. *Rochester Sun*, 7 June 1925.

2. USNA, United States Coast Guard Annual Report for 1925, pp. 12-13.

3. USNA, Customs Seizures, Box 1959, 1922–1931.

4. Don Harrison, op. cit.

5. Rochester *Democrat and Chronicle*, 28 August 1925.

6. The evidence that Thompson was working for Kerr and that the *Sparkley* was Kerr's boat is circumstantial. An article in the *Rochester Democrat and Chronicle* speculated that Thompson was probably connected to the "King of the Lake Runners". Thompson gave his address as 24 Concession Street in Hamilton, a vacant lot, suggesting he knew Concession Street well. There were many Thompsons in Hamilton, but not many living in that part of the city. There was a Thompson who worked in the rolling mills near the Bay View Hotel. Dillon, the owner, was a bootlegger supplied by Kerr. He may have suggested Thompson to Kerr as a possible recruit to help Alf Wheat. The *Sparkley*'s size and black colour fit the description of one of Kerr's boats supplied by Kelly Thompson, a neighbour and sporting associate of Kerr. Several sources note that Kerr's boats were always painted black as was the *Sparkley*. Also, the coast guard arrest report notes that the smugglers anchored the boat out from shore, a tactic followed by Kerr.

7. *Rochester Democrat and Chronicle*, 24 September 1925. Also, USNA, letter dated 16 February 1928, to the United States Attorney General from Richard R. Templeton, U.S. Attorney for the Western District of New York.

8. USNA, Coast Guard Records, M.B. McCune's arrest report of 12 November 1925.

9. Ibid, Department of Justice, Rochester, New York, 5 March 1926. This document sets out the charges against Kerr. There is no longer any record of the extradition proceedings but it is mentioned by various people interviewed, and in the *Mail and Empire*, 27 July 1926.

10. *Hamilton Herald*, 5 December 1925.

Twelve: Hockey and Homicide

1. Interview, Dan "Mickey" Ward, 14 January 1993.

2. *Hamilton Spectator*, 27 February 1926.

3. Ibid, 11 & 18 March, 1926.

4. *Hamilton Spectator*, 25 March.

5. Ibid, 29 March 1926.

6. The information on the *Pollywog* is derived from a number of sources including: Jack Morris Jr., who helped to build it, and sailed in it for three years. Purtell Quick, a life-long commercial fisherman, who knew Kerr and told me that the *Pollywog* was not very sturdy. Newspaper references to the boat, at the time of the search for Kerr and the *Pollywog*, confirm the size of the engines, the boat's speed, and its length. Morris was able to confirm these facts, although the *Pollywog's* maximum speed varies from one source to another, 40 MPH (65 km/h) is most often quoted.

7. USNA, Coast Guard Arrest Report, 19 July 1926.

8. Ibid.

9. Interview, Bill Lynch, Belleville, 11 March 1983.

10. PAO, Poison Liquor Files, 1926.

11. *Hamilton Spectator*, 26 July 1926.

Thirteen: Cross-Border Crime

James Dubro and Robin Rowland's book on Rocco Perri was a useful source of information on Perri's connections to U.S. criminals and to James Lavallée.

1. Annual Report of the O.P.P. for 1923.

2. *Hamilton Spectator*, 30 July 1926.

3. AO, poison liquor file, RG4 C-3.

4. AO, RG4 C-3, a letter from the Criminal Investigation Department, New Scotland Yard, sets out the details of their attempt to intercept Sottile when he landed at Liverpool. It is clear that they had their man.

5. Toronto *Star*, 7 August 1926.

6. *The Globe*, 9 August 1926.

7. Toronto *Star*, 28 August 1926.

8. *Hamilton Spectator*, 4 December 1926.

9. *Daily Intelligencer*, 21 December 1926.

Fourteen: Bootleggers, Politicians, and Clergymen

1. *Hamilton Spectator*, 2 December 1926.

2. *Daily Intelligencer*, 16 February 1923.

3. *Financial Post*, 11 January 1924.

4. Interview, Court Miller, Belleville, 30 September 1983.

5. *Daily Intelligencer*, 11 September 1924. Ackerill's office was located in what are now the offices of the law firm of Brady, Cort, and Meninga.

6. *Daily Intelligencer*, 14 October 1924.

7. AO.

8. *Daily Intelligencer*, 27 October 1924.

9. *Daily Intelligencer*, 20 November 1924.

10. Picton *Gazette*, 30 October 1924.

11. *Toronto Star*, 27 May 1925.

12. *Toronto Star*, 20 June 1925.

13. *Daily Intelligencer*, 19 October 1926.

14. *Toronto Star*, 15 May 1926.

15. *Daily Intelligencer*, 22 November 1926.

16. *Hamilton Spectator*, 26 November 1926.

17. *Daily Intelligencer*, 17 November 1926.

18. *Telegram*, 11 December 1926.

19. Peter Oliver, *G. Howard Ferguson, Ontario Tory*. University of Toronto Press, Toronto, 1977, pp. 272-273.

Fifteen: Courts and Commissioners

1. *Hamilton Spectator*, 11 and 13 December 1926; also *Globe*, 13 December 1926.

2. Interview, Bill Lynch, op. cit.

3. *Daily Intelligencer*, 2 November 1927.

4. *Hamilton Spectator*, 30 December 1926.

5. Interview, Jack Morris Jr., Hamilton, 8 December 1983.

6. Interview, John Carey, Picton, 29 March 1983.

7. *Daily Intelligencer*, 20 August 1926, and 26 May 1927.

8. *Toronto Star*, 18 November 1927.

9. USNA, Coast Guard files are extensive on the *Uncas*, and include a detailed description of the vessel, a photocopy of a picture, and a valuation of $50,000.

10. *Daily Intelligencer* 17 June 1927, and the *Oswego Palladium Times*, 15 June 1927.

11. Interview, Jack Morris Jr., Hamilton, op. cit.

Sixteen: The Quebec Connection

1. NA Memo of George Gregg Miller, dated 31 July 1930.

192   Notes

2. Toronto *Star*, 1 March 1929.

3. *Daily Intelligencer*, 27 August 1926.

4. Interview, Jim "Snipe" Mathews, Belleville, 12 March 1994.

5. USNA, H.T. Nugent, letter of 12 December 1928.

6. Interview, Ken McConnell, 22 January 1983. Also *Daily Intelligencer*, 6 October 1928.

7. Interview, John B. Kerr, nephew of Kerr, Hamilton, 27 September 1993.

Seventeen: Whisky and Ice

Information for this chapter was derived from interviews with Purtell Quick, Jack Morris Jr., Ken Leavens, Aaron McGlennon, Fred Wilkinson, and Len and Elizabeth Wheat. The information on the search for the *Pollywog* is derived in part from these interviews and from the following newspapers: *Kingston Whig Standard*- 5, 19, 21, 22, 23, 26, 28, of March, and 1 April; *Daily Ontario* (Belleville) – 5, 6, 13, 18, 28, 30, of March and 19 April; *Cobourg Star*-2 April; *Brighton Ensign* – 15, 29, of March; and *Picton Gazette* – 6, 13, 16, 20, 23, 27, of March and 3 April 1929.

1. *Hamilton Spectator*, 12 May 1927.

2. USNA, Court records for Western District of New York, Dockets 1540 B, and 11066.

3. Wright, Gerald, "Someone had to keep the rumrunners' cars running," *Canadian Automotive Trade Magazine*, September 1972, pp. 41-42.

4. *Kingston Whig Standard*, 21 March 1929.

5. *Kingston Whig Standard*, 22 March 1929.

6. Aaron McGlennon, Cobourg, 9 September 1993.

Eighteen: Murder or Misadventure?

United States Coast Guard files from the U.S. National Archives provide detailed information on the *Uncas*. Interviews with Jack and Milt Staud, descendants of the notorious Midge Staud, and U.S. Coast Guard reports of encounters with the *Dorthy* were used to determine when the *Dorthy* first appeared on Lake Ontario.

A Selected Bibliography

Dubro, James, and Rowland, Robin F. *King of the Mob, Rocco Perri and the Women Who Ran His Rackets*. Penguin Books Canada Ltd., 1987.

Higley, Dahn D. *The History of the Ontario Provincial Police Force*. Queen's Printer, Toronto, 1984.

Humphries, Charles W. *Honest Enough to Be Bold, The Life and Times of Sir James Whitney*. University of Toronto Press, Toronto, London, Buffalo, 1985.

Hunt, C.W. *Booze, Boats, and Billions*. McClelland and Stewart, Toronto, 1988.

Jarret, Thomas. *The Evolution of Trenton, Ontario, 1813-1913*. Published by author, Trenton, 1913.

Johnston, Charles. *E.C. Drury: Agrarian Idealist*. University of Toronto Press, Toronto, Buffalo, London, 1986.

Manners and Rules of Good Society, or Solecisms to Be Avoided. By a member of the Aristocracy. London and New York. Fredrick Warne and Company, 1913.

Nicholson, Colonel G.W.L. *Official History of the Canadian Army, in the First World War, Canadian Expeditionary Force 1914-1919*. Ministry of National Defence, Ottawa, 1964.

United Association of Journeymen and Apprentices of the Plumbing and Pipe Fitting Industry, Local 67. *Organized for Action, 90th Anniversary, 1899-1989, Local 67, Hamilton, Ontario*. A booklet published by the union, Hamilton, 1989.

Pettigrew, Eileen. *The Silent Enemy, Canada and the Deadly Flu Epidemic of 1918*. Western Producer Prairie Books, Saskatoon, 1983.

Tennyson, Brian D. "Sir William Hearst and the Ontario Temperance Act." *Ontario History*, Volume 55, 1963.

Tennyson, Brian D. "The War and Votes for Women." *Ontario History*, Volume 57, 1965.

Weaver, John C. *Hamilton: An Illustrated History*. James Lorimer and Company, and National Museum of Man, Toronto, 1982.